Best wishes

[signature] John Reed

June 2018

BACK IN TIME

JOHN REED

First publication in Great Britain

For Angela, Ellen and Richard

Thanks to Peter Watson, Bob Beattie, Nick, Barrie, Holly, Dave Robson, Eric Punshon, Davy Whittaker for the great photos and all the lovely people I had the chance to work with over those magic years.

Prologue

It was July 1966 and just another night at the Europa Tanzdiele, a club situated in the German University town of Marburg. Set on the river Lahn with its nearest town Frankfurt, it was a town very much steeped in history and full of young German boys and girls pursuing their further education. Needless to say, we were happy to pursue the girls and cement Anglo-German relations; we were falling in love with the Fräuleins on a regular basis. It was the swinging sixties and British groups dominated the German club scene, travelling up and down the autobahns in clapped out vans. None more clapped out than ours! The English bands played one month residencies at the myriad of clubs which had sprung up all over Germany. Inspired, no doubt, by the success of the Star Club and Top Ten Clubs in Hamburg which had become legendary. Somehow we had got booked here in the third month of our first German tour. Although not on the main circuit of clubs, the agent had told us it was a good club and very popular with the locals. As the town was full of students, we thought it filled in a month and certainly saved us having to go back to the UK. This was our first adventure abroad and we were living like a real professional group, fulfilling the dreams we all had, dreaming we would 'make it' as musicians.

Marburg, close to the Black Forest, was not only home to lots of students, but also home to many Romany gypsies. I will never forget this particular night sitting behind the drum kit, half way through our second set, whilst the locals danced their hearts out, I spotted some commotion coming from the left hand side of the club close to the entrance. In a moment, around 50 gypsies bearing guns, knives and knuckle dusters burst into the club and began to form a semi circle round the stage. I scanned the line of swarthy faces and the total look of menace on each and every one of them was enough to fill anyone with fear. I felt the cold stream of sweat run down my back with sheer terror as we realised it was us they were looking for. Events the night before had determined our fate tonight. As usual, our keyboard player Malcolm and his ever busy appendage had been involved. If only he could keep it in his pants for five minutes we might have had half a chance. The other guys in the group exchanged worried glances and Peter the bass player, standing close to me at the back of the stage turned and said 'What the fuck do we do know'? The expression on my face obviously told him I had no answer. How appropriate that at that moment in time we were playing 'Somebody Help Me' by The Spencer Davies Group. It was one of our favourite tunes and suited our style. After playing twenty verses and several extra choruses the number eventually had to come to an end and our second set was over. We reluctantly made our way off the stage for a break and the mob of gypsies advanced to the side of the stage. They were intent on revenge and there wasn't much room with all of them crowding into the small space. Their leader was at the front of the mob and speaking heatedly to Arnde, our German road manager. The sweat forming on Arnde's forehead indicated that things were very bad. I honestly thought this was the end of my life. How had four young lads from Sunderland in the North East of England come to this? It looked like there was no way out; certainly escape was not an option as there were no emergency doors behind the stage. Only solid Teutonic walls that a Panzer tank would have difficulty breaching. The journey to this nightmare and this whole sorry adventure had begun in much happier circumstances 17 years earlier in the North East of England.

Chapter One

I arrived in this world on the 15th January 1948 at The General Hospital in Sunderland around 11.30 in the morning. I am reliably informed my mother Joyce tucked into a hearty lunch after her exertions and I guess I slept to recover from the trauma of being so rudely interrupted from the vastly more comfortable surroundings of my mother's womb. I can assure you that Sunderland in January is somewhere a polar bear would find suitable as a habitat. My father, Lawrence, was in the merchant navy and he was away when I was born. I actually didn't see very much of him in my formative years, as he would be away for months on end and then be home for around two weeks and then he would be gone again. He was a Chief Refrigeration Engineer with Royal Mail Lines, who ran passenger cargo ships to South America. The ships would bring back Argentinean beef back to the UK and also pick up fruit from the Canary Islands on route back home. He told me that when he qualified as an Engineer being away at sea paid more than working on land and this had persuaded him to take that particular employment path. Money was tight in those days and the extra pay was much needed. We shared a house in the High Barnes area of Sunderland with my mother's parents, George and Caroline Graham. They were surrogate parents to me. Mum worked at the General Hospital as a State Registered Nurse, something she was always very proud of and went on to be a nursing sister. She was of the old school of nursing and I can still remember the crispness of her uniform and starched collars and cuffs. It just seemed so wonderfully clean. In the days before duvets, my mother's nursing skills were brought home when she used to change the sheets on our beds. They were so well made it was almost impossible to get into the bed, as the sheets and blankets were so tightly folded into the mattress!

Post war Sunderland was a thriving town, most famous in those days for its ship building, mining and not to forget its football team – 'The Black Cats'. The town, situated either side of the river Wear, was home to some of the biggest shipyards in the world. Laing's, Doxford's, Steel's and Austin & Pickersgill produced some of the most impressive ships launched of their time. The cranes dominated the skyline along the river and there was a hive of activity each day as the shipwrights carried out their work. It was always a big occasion when a ship was due to be launched and the town almost came to a standstill. I would often cycle down to Pallion and watch the activity on the river. Seeing a big ship take shape was magical to a young lad like me. Throughout Sunderland's long and impressive history, its survival and commerce was based on the industry situated on the North and South of the river Wear. The locals were always saying we 'mac' (make) it here and 'tac' (take) it ou'er there. So whatever was made north of the Wear got sent south and vice versa. Hence the local residents of Sunderland became known over the years as 'Maccams'. The shipyards always took their holiday at the same time during the summer, as it was more practical to shut the whole thing down. The holiday was the last week in July and the first week of August. It was known locally as the 'shipyard fortnight'. All the hundreds of workers would be off at the same time.

In the days before continental holidays and cheap air travel were the norm, families flocked to Roker and Seaburn, Sunderland's twin seaside resorts, to spend their holiday time there. The beaches were very sandy and the tide went out a long way. Playing on the beach was lots of fun and very safe. It was the typical childhood idyll. Once we were there, a million adventures would unfold which we would enact, lost in the limitless imagination of childhood fantasies. The big treat was always Notorianni's ice cream, they were legendary Italian ice cream makers and it was like a pilgrimage to their ice cream parlour for a '99'. When extra funds were available, the fun fair was at hand with its thrills and spills. Always the highlight was the dodgems and a chance to show off your driving skills. The car jockeys, young lads paid to collect the money from the punters and generally look after the cars, spent their time hanging on to the back of the cars that were occupied by pretty young girls. They would spin the cars round whereupon the girls concerned would scream and look terrified. This was supposed to impress them enough to want to come back for another ride and be a potential date for the jockey concerned. Usually it resulted in the girls turning green and puking up the chips and candy floss they had eaten earlier.

I spent many happy days on the beach at Roker. I used to get the bus to see my cousin Paul. They lived in Birmingham, but would come up to visit Paul's grand parents during the summer school holidays. His grand parents had a house on Roker Avenue and you could see all the fishing boats going out to sea from their back bedroom. Paul and I would spend hours just watching all the activity on the river. It had a magic about it that fascinated two young boys ready for adventure. On summer mornings, we would set off to an area on the sea front at Roker which had cliffs 60 feet high. These cliffs were known as the 'Cat & Dog Steps'. We would start building a series of dams to keep the water in the rock pools that had collected as the tide receded. It was back breaking work keeping the walls shored up. As the morning progressed, the sand would dry out and families would appear spreading out their towels and picnics ready for a day of leisure. As early afternoon approached, Paul and I would abandon the maintenance of the sandy dams and retreat to the safety of the upper promenade. Nature would eventually take its course and the dams would break, disgorging gallons of sea water in the direction of these poor families spread far and wide across the beach. We thought it was hilarious, but the families did not share our sense of humour and we would have to disappear fast as angry parents came looking for the culprits. I guess these days we would have been early candidates for an ASBO.

Sunderland, apart from ship building, was also part of the great Durham coalfield and there were many mining villages for miles around. Each village was built around the colliery and they were always very close communities. Each village was very self-contained with the colliery providing employment for the men, a school, church, Co-Op shop and of course at least two clubs to provide them with entertainment. It was understandable that in such austere times, the local population saw no need to venture much further than their own village; it had everything they needed. For a special day, a trip to Sunderland or Durham would be something to look forward to. Sunderland was always busy and apart from the buses, it also had trams that traversed the town. Binns Department Store was the place to be seen and having a coffee in their restaurant on a Saturday morning was a must. Vaux was the locally brewery and used magnificent dray horses to deliver their beer to the local town pubs.

Chapter Two

Our family life was centred round Ewesley Road Methodist church in the High Barnes area. Every Sunday I was dispatched there morning, afternoon and night. Morning consisted of the Young Worshipper's League, Sunday school in the afternoon and the evening service at 6.30pm. It was a heavy religious day for a young lad. However, with a careful bit of fiddling, I managed to keep a small percentage of my collection money, which financed my love of sweets. I figured being so religious had to have some benefits and I was sure God wouldn't mind. I prayed quite often and would always ask God if he minded. I took his lack of reply as a silent approval, although I was never quite sure if these misdemeanours would be entered into the 'big book' and held against me when I met my maker. Mum was a keen member of the church choir, as was my grandfather, so music was ever present in the house. It seemed that every household in those days had an upright piano and the sound of Mum tinkling away in the front room singing some oratorio was a common sound. I always thought the choir were lucky, as they seemed to have privileged seats to the left of the church and it was easy for them to slip out during the sermon. I am sure my grandfather took advantage of this to have a quiet cigarette. I can picture him now standing outside the side door, Woodbine in hand enjoying the smoke before returning to the choir stalls. In those days, tipped cigarettes were unusual and certainly not to be smoked by men. Being rather 'canny' my grandfather would smoke the cigarette down as far as it would go (waste not, want not!). The result of this was he would have an orange nicotine stained top lip, which we all thought was hilarious.

My first taste of education was at Barnes Junior School, just five minutes walk from our house. It was a happy time and like most five year olds, didn't have a care in the world. Life was sweet and uncomplicated. Then one Christmas I contracted measles and simultaneously got a bad cold. The combination can be dangerous and I was put in isolation in our front room. She relates how she had to change to sheets on the bed twice a day and when she lifted them off me, the steam rose off my body due to my high temperature. Thanks to my mother's good nursing I got through it, but it left me with Asthma. It was not diagnosed as such in those days and it was assumed I had bronchitis. I didn't have the luxury of puffers as they do now, and can remember leaning my face against the cold school wall wondering where my next breath was coming from. This had a huge impact on my sport and my enjoyment of it, as I just couldn't run for any distance. I absolutely hated football because of this. I couldn't run for any distance without gasping for breath, so I got stuck in goal. Winters in the North East in those days were like Alaska and when the North East wind blew in off the sea it could cut you in two. To make matters worse, the football pitches we played on were on the top of Barnes Hill. It was massively exposed to the elements and not a trace of a wind breaker anywhere. On many occasions I thought it had cut me in two as the ball sailed past my frozen torso for another conceded goal. I remember we used to toss for colours or white shirts. The coloured shirts were rugby style and quite warm, whereas the white shirts were just ordinary school shirts. We always seem to get white and no posh goalie shirt for me either.

I was also sent to piano lessons at Mr. Cooper's who lived in our street. I hated every minute of it. I tried as hard as I could, but I just couldn't master the instrument. How I envy those lucky people now, who can slip on to a piano stool and let their fingers stroll across the keyboard playing some melody as if it was the most natural thing for any human being to do. I was determined to keep the musical tradition in the family going, but it wasn't going to be the piano. My dad's father, Jack Reed, give me his violin. However, rather than pursue this fine instrument, I dispensed with the bow and used to play it like a ukulele. Needless to say, the instrument did not last very long having been so abused.

My piano lessons came to an abrupt end as fate took a hand – almost quite literally. One day I returned home from school and, unusually there was no one at home. I was desperate to get my bike out and go play with my friends in Barnes Park, our regular after school meeting place. There had to be a way into the house and I was sure I could do it. Downstairs, our house had a bay window and the side windows were the old fashioned sash type that would slide up and down. I noticed that one of them was not locked properly, so I proceeded to try and push the window upwards. Unfortunately my hand pushing up the window was in the middle of the glass pane. Just as the window started to move the glass cracked and my hand went straight through the glass severing my wrist. The cut was very deep and I could see the bone, which was not the best of sights for a ten year old. There was blood everywhere on the front path and my cries alerted a neighbour who quickly came to my rescue. She wrapped a towel round the wound and applied pressure to ease the bleeding.

They then called my mother, who worked at the hospital only five minutes walk from the house. I could see her running up the street to attend to her son whose impatience had very nearly brought his musical and sporting career to an early close. It didn't take her long to realise hospital treatment was needed and we walked over to the General Hospital so a doctor could look it over. We were then told, much to my mother's annoyance, that they couldn't treat me there and we would have to go to the Royal Infirmary. This was close to the town centre and we had to wait for a public bus which took us to the Infirmary. Bearing in mind the nature of the wound, public transport was not ideal. By this time the shock had worn off, and the wound was now hurting like hell. We arrived at the Infirmary and after a short wait, were seen by another Doctor. It was pronounced that I had cut the tendons in my thumb and after a temporary stitch was inserted, with great pain and tears, we were sent off to the Accident and Emergency Hospital at Monkwearmouth, north of Sunderland town centre. Another bloody journey by public transport! This was becoming the longest Friday in my entire life. My Mother, by this time, was beginning to lose the unswerving faith she had held in the National Health Service which she had served so well and defended all her life.

Shortly after we arrived and checked in, we were finally seen by a surgeon who insisted I was operated on that night. I was prepped and ready to go within the hour and they operated on the wrist that night. I awoke later to discover a large plaster cast on my left arm and hand with my thumb erect. It felt very sore inside and I eventually drifted off to sleep hoping the pain killers would kick in.

My Mother collected me the following day at lunch time. Thankfully she had persuaded my uncle to pick me up in his car as we had had enough bus journeys. I was only allowed to go home then, as my mother was a nurse and could administer the penicillin injections I had to have for the following ten days. I think if my mother had realised what this entailed, she would have left me there!

The injections had to be given intramuscularly in the backside, so the needle had to be quite long to penetrate the flesh and then into the muscle. Well, when I got first sight of this bloody big syringe, I legged it all round the house. My poor mother ended up chasing me from one room to another trying to administer this course of antibiotics. She eventually reasoned with me that if she didn't do it, I would have to go back to hospital and have some hideous old battleaxe of a Sister do it. She won. As the days went on, even though she alternated from one buttock to another, they got very sore and became increasingly painful. How glad was I when the course finished, but I think my mother was rather more pleased than I was to end the ordeal. I remember my Grandmother would disappear when it was time to have them administered, I think it upset her too much to hear me cry.

Ten days later I had the cast off and by this time the skin had grown over the stitches. More pain, as they were dragged out of the wound. I vowed then that I would not go near another stupid sash window as long as I lived. I never returned to piano lessons after that, a decision I regret now, but at the time it seemed like an escape from hell.

Gradually normal service resumed in the hand and the extra care and attention I had been afforded seemed to be diminishing. Days and nights were spent in the parlour downstairs where my grandparents lived. Saturday afternoons we were sat round the huge valve radio listening to BBC Sport's Report with all the football results and its legendary theme tune. Saturday evenings we would watch the Billy Cotton Band Show and I would sneak under the table to become invisible so I wouldn't be packed off to bed. In those early days I would lie spell bound under the table listening to Yana sing 'Climb Up The Garden Wall' with her sexy cleavage tumbling over some tight frock. It was obvious something in me was climbing up somewhere as her voice begged me personally to join her for some intimate company. Amazing what a 14" black and white television could evoke in a young teenage boy. As the hand got back to normal, being waited on hand and foot ceased and it was chores as usual. Being left handed I couldn't do homework for around six weeks which was another bonus, but in hindsight may have had an adverse effect on my school work as shortly after that I failed my 11 plus exam.

Chapter Three

When the brown window envelope dropped through the door of 24 Ewesley Road, Sunderland, I am sure they heard it land on the door mat a thousand miles away. It seemed to hang in the air for hours and then suddenly drop with a bang as it hit the floor behind the front door. It could, of course, have been the Littlewoods catalogue that came with it. Like all things important in the North, everyone assembled in the front room. It was this awful ritual that everyone did when things of importance were either being said or revealed. The front room seemed to give the occasion more majesty. If it was good enough for the best china it was good enough to announce my exam results.

It certainly gave me the shits, as I was not optimistic at the outcome. The envelope was duly opened and Mother started to read it. As the words left her lips it all started to become a haze. In and out of the haze came the words 'unfortunately' and 'sorry' as my heart sank to my boots. 'This is a disaster for the family' was my mother's first words. I had brought shame on the family by failing the exam that would have led me through the golden gates of academic heaven known as Bede School. This was the popular grammar school that all decent achievers were meant to go to and I had failed. I felt as though I had committed a murder. The mood of the house the rest of the day was sombre and mumbled conversations could be heard in the parlour, to which I was not privy to their content.

To her credit, my Mother picked herself up soon afterwards and resolved that somehow she would find the money to send me to a private grammar school. She was not having me going to some secondary school. I realise now that it was hard for the family, when so many of the children whose parents attended the church, were going to Bede School and I wasn't. There was such a stigma in those days if you failed and it left an unfair blemish which seemed to mark you for life if you didn't have a grammar school education. Thank goodness the 11 plus is no longer with us.

After sitting the entrance examination, which as I remember I did not do too well in maths, I was first sent to Neville's Cross Grammar School in Durham City. Obviously the thought of my future school fees glossed over my mathematic inadequacies. This was quite some journey for an 11 year old. There was a two mile walk from home to the bus stop and then a 12 mile bus journey into Durham and a good half mile walk from the bus station to the school up a very steep hill. It was at this school that I got my first taste of Europe. In 1959, European travel was not as it is today, so when the school organised a weekend trip to Oostende, it felt like we were going to the other side of the world. A coach journey from Durham down to Dover was bad enough, but then a ferry crossing the Channel, seemed like we were leaving civilisation behind. I was given a bedroom with three other pupils who happened to be on the first floor of the hotel. It also had a flat roof garage under the window, which was a convenient escape route for the older pupil's intent on going into town and getting drunk. We had a great time and a few of us managed to get the odd bottle of Pilsner and a packet of cigarettes to help us through the nights. I do remember spending a lot of time on the beach and reflecting how far away England seemed to be.

Not much sleep was had by any of us on that trip, as the steady flow of drunken pupils made their way to and from the local hostelry through our room each night. The ferry back was very choppy and by the time we embarked on the coach to take us back to Durham, we were all quite green. Choppy seas mixed with greasy chips, illicit booze and cigarettes. We very quickly learned this did not make for a good mixture. The master in charge of us used most of the expensive Eau de Cologne he had bought as a present to hide the smell of vomit at the back of the bus. Magic!

The best part of this short year at Neville's Cross was going to the park opposite the school. As soon as the bell went for lunch, I would grab my packed lunch and make my way with a couple of friends across the road to the park. It was high on a hill and overlooked Durham railway station. The highlight every day was the excitement of seeing the 'Flying Scotsman' roar through the station; it was sheer magic. I wasn't that interested in trains as such, but the Mallard Class steam engines of their day had an aura about them that made them very special. I had started smoking by now and took delight in sitting on top of the hill lighting up a Passing Cloud cigarette which we regarded as super cool. They were Turkish and had different coloured papers, oval in shape and tasted quite strong as the tobacco was toasted for extra flavour. I don't know how we got away with it then, but on last period, when it got to about ten minutes before the bell went, we would slowly pack our bags, slip our coats on so that when the bell went it was a stampede out of the classroom, down the stairs three at a time and a mad run to the bus station in Durham city to get the early bus. Missing that meant a half hour delay which was a pain on the occasions the teacher would hold us back.

One morning, I got up as usual and came bounding down the stairs into the parlour to tuck into breakfast before going off to Durham. Mum was sitting by herself; it was obvious she had been crying. I was confused and worried at what tragedy had befallen us. She explained that during the night, Grandma

Caroline had had a heart attack and died. She was laid out in the front room and Grandpa Graham was in their bed. It was a wonderful old feather bed type that always seemed to be more comfortable than the modern divan to a ten year old. I remember climbing in beside him and giving him a cuddle. He didn't cry. He just lay there all quiet and calmed his grandson, who had just had his first experience of death. He was the most amazing man. I think so many of that generation were supreme people. Their values and way of life were so much more uncomplicated. Perhaps because they had lived through austere times and two world wars, they appreciated everything good, as they had also experienced the bad times too.

During the First World War he had been a rigger in the Royal Flying Corps, the pre-runner to the RAF, and had looked after the flying ace Albert Ball. He used to tell me tales of how the planes would arrive in tea chests and they would have to assemble then from a kit. They even had big type rubber bands which acted as the suspension. He never stopped being amazed how they actually flew, never mind shooting down the Hun. From that experience to watching Concorde take off is quite something to comprehend in one lifetime. The funeral took place a few days later and the Church was packed to the rafters. Caroline was well loved by so many and the turn out confirmed how much.

Things changed shortly after that at home as it was decided to make the house one instead of us living upstairs and Grandpa downstairs. I was now to have the luxury of my own bedroom as up until then my bed had been in my parent's room. That must have had its moments! I remember once finding an oblong box under my parent's bed. I opened it up and to my horror realised it was a condom. It was called 'The Paragon Sheath'. It was reusable and after washing it out, you coated it in French chalk to keep it dry. How one could be romantic with a Paragon Sheath is beyond me. It looked like the inner tube from a lorry's tyre. No wonder I was an only child! I was very happy to be moving and all round it was much better. What had been our kitchen became my bedroom.

The travelling to Durham was not suiting me or the family, so attention was turned to finding a school nearer to home. After some research and general enquiries, it was decided I would go to Argyle House Grammar School in Ashbrooke. Ashbrooke was a nice suburb of Sunderland and a ten minute bike ride from home. This was much better for me, although the green uniform with caps that had yellow half moons on either side did not impress me at all. It was a High Church of England school and many of the masters wore black cassocks which gave them a very austere look about them. Discipline was harsh and the cane was administered with great regularity. I remember in my first week going to get something from the library without permission. I was summoned before the headmaster to explain my actions. I apologised and said 'I thought I was allowed to do that'. The headmaster, Father Gott, who was later imprisoned for child molesting, looked at me from behind his thick glasses which made his eyes look like tiny beads replied 'Laddy, the only thing you are allowed to do in this school is breathe, and that is with special permission'! The school motto was 'Labor Omnia Vincit' – 'Work Conquers All'. As far as I was concerned, it might as well have said 'Abandon Hope All Who Enter Here'.

On one occasion I was beaten so badly, the bruises on my buttocks were so severe I could hardly walk. I had struggled home on my bike and arrived home late as a result. My mother knew something was amiss even though I was keeping out of her way. I didn't want to admit I had been caned, but she eventually got it out of me. She examined me and was horrified at what she saw. She got a friend of ours, Jim Gray, who was a police sergeant, to witness the injuries. She then sent a very serious note to the school the following day mentioning that the police had seen the injuries. No reply was ever received but I never got caned again after that. Obviously the Headmaster got some sadistic pleasure in this and the extra activities that used to take place at the headmaster's house under the guise of 'choir practice' at St. Hilda's in Sunderland were not to be discovered for some years to come. My mother had a feeling something wasn't right and kept me well away from there. One thing that came out of my time at Argyle House was I discovered cricket. It was perfect for me as it involved more sprinting as opposed to running constantly and I could at least get my breath back.

I became quite good and got into the school first XI. It was a bit of an ordeal going to play matches as the school played at Boldon Cricket Club on Wednesday afternoons. Boldon was halfway to Newcastle so I had to get a bus from the town centre through to Boldon. I had to go changed, so I had my whites on, cap and blazer and was the subject of much derision from the local hooligans. Anyone playing cricket in Sunderland in the 50's was regarded as a complete 'poof' as football was like a religion. My grandfather took me to Roker Park on several occasions but I didn't really enjoy it. There was no such thing as all seater stadiums and for a little lad standing in the Roker end being swayed from one direction to another by the crowd with his feet off the ground was very claustrophobic and scary.

Chapter Four

It was at this time that music was starting to stir something inside me. A couple of boys at school had bought semi acoustic guitars and stuck electric pick ups on them. After school, they would practice in the common room plugging them into an old amplifier. I was just hooked on the twangy sound they made and wanted more than anything to play guitar. This seemed the way to go for me and it was much sexier than the piano. At least that's what I thought at the time.

A friend who lived in our street had made me an old crystal radio set. My Uncle Bill had been in the RAF during the war and he had left an old pair of headphones from his aircraft in the downstairs pantry. I was well set. Into bed and under the bed clothes I went. On with the Biggle's headphones and down with the big switch to get power. I was transported to another world courtesy of Radio Luxembourg. The magic 208 metres medium wave – The Station of the Stars was their slogan. The station was based in the Grand Duchy of Luxembourg and they played endless great rock n' roll records and the popular music of the day. Unbelievably, the BBC did not and considered pop and rock to be a passing fashion that would quickly go away. Going on air at 7pm was just about when we would be sent off to bed. The golden voices of Jack Jackson, David Gell, Pete Murray and Sam Costa, telling us all about the great stars who made the records. I saved up some pocket money and bought an old guitar from a second hand shop in Chester Road. It was almost physically impossible to play as the strings were so far away from the fret board. I struggled on through the pain barrier until I could manage a reasonable three chords. I couldn't get enough of it. One day at Argyle House, I was dragged into the common room by some sixth formers who had heard that I could play guitar. I was thrown into a seat and given a guitar and told to play. I managed one verse of 'Come on Everybody' by Eddie Cochran before I was thrown out and kicked down the stairs. I think they obviously felt I wasn't a threat to their band, as I was not asked to perform for them again. So ended my first audition.

My parents had bought a new Dansette record player for the lounge. My mother had bought records by Kathleen Ferrier, a classical contralto who Mum wanted to emulate and the soundtrack LP of 'South Pacific'. I went off to town and the first records I purchased were 'April Love' by Pat Boone and 'King Creole' by Elvis. I played them over and over again and completely got hooked on the sounds. With having only two records to play, the B-sides also got a hammering. Flip side of King Creole was a song called 'Crawfish' and

Pat Boone sang 'When the Swallows Come Back to Capistrano'. I remember when I went to the record store to buy them; I was asked if I wanted the 78 rpm or the new 45 rpm? I looked at the tiny 45 rpm and opted for the 78 rpm, as to me you got more for your money!

It was around this time that I started to go to the Church youth club which happened every Friday night from 7pm until 10.30. I had managed to get hold of a small Elpico amplifier to go with my guitar and eventually upgraded the guitar to a sold electric Burns guitar. I was, certainly in my own mind, Sunderland's answer to Duane Eddy. Every Friday night I would be there with my amp on top of the piano boring everyone with the same old tunes of 'Peter Gun' and 'Shazam' which ventured no further than the fifth and sixth strings of my guitar. I also used to take our record player with me and when my fingers and the people could no longer take any more Duane Eddy, I would play the half dozen records I had in my collection. It was on one of these nights as I was giving Peter Gun yet another outing that the youth club doors swung open and in walked two guys. One had a guitar under his arm and the other was travelling light. I eyed them with great suspicion as they approached. The two guys were George Gibbon and Bob Beattie. George, the guitar carrying interloper, asked if he could plug into my amp. With great reluctance I agreed and he started playing all these chords to my very erratic playing.

I did not want to leave my ground and almost turned red with pain as my bladder filled to capacity. Eventually I had to take my leave for a call of nature. Bob asked me if he could borrow my guitar whilst I was away. Instinctively I knew I was doomed from that moment on. On my return from the toilet, George and Bob had turned into Hank Marvin and Bruce Welch from the Shadows. Their musical prowess on the guitar was way ahead of me and I didn't even have the inclination to ask for my guitar back. They had also attracted a large amount of girls who were now hanging around the piano.

The same area had been strangely empty when I was playing! I found myself tapping and keeping a beat on the piano top. A voice inside my head said 'Johnny Boy, if you don't learn another instrument quick, you are not going to be in this band'. The night broke up and despite my disappointment, I had been exhilarated by the live sounds we had created in that little corner of the club. We agreed to meet the following Friday and I set to work acquiring some drums. I put some feelers out and someone who lived a few streets away had an old set of drums they no longer used. I managed to persuade my mother to stump up the money and the drums were mine. My mother was brilliant to me with things like this. I would always get a lecture about how I had to look after them etc but she would always come up with the goods. She was a real hero. The kit was as basic as you could get. It comprised a Beverley Bass Drum and pedal, a Carlton Cracker snare drum and stand, one cymbal and stand and a 12" Premier tom tom. It had no floor tom tom and no hi-hat.

That week, I practised playing along to records on the old Dansette record player. To my surprise, I took to the drums quite well and by the end of the week could at least knock out a beat. The following Friday arrived and it was Youth Club time. I was quite excited now and the next problem I had to overcome was transport. I could carry the guitar and small amp down the street but the drums were a bigger handful. I managed to borrow a friend's old pram and balanced the kit on this and set off. It must have been quite a sight seeing me pushing this old pram piled high with the drums balanced precariously on the old frame. Thankfully I only had to get it down the end of the street but I managed. I always made a point of doing this early, as I didn't think it looked very cool.

The first sessions went well and already we were gelling into quite a decent outfit. We realised we needed a bass player to complete the line up and within weeks we had recruited Clive and we were on our way. The repertoire of the group to start off with was strictly instrumentals and only a couple of songs. It was all Shadows, the Ventures and Duane Eddy at first with some Eddie Cochrane and Cliff tunes at the end. It was quite funny to see the solitary microphone placed in the middle of the stage like some alien being. It didn't take us long to realise that the audience reacted much more to vocal numbers and slowly our repertoire changed to almost all vocals. We were lucky that Bob had a very good voice as it turned out and he handled all the lead vocals while George and I would do harmonies.

As the weeks went by, our repertoire grew into a full set and it was getting to the point where we were going to have to choose a name for the group. Hours were spent mulling over dictionaries, books and lots of brainstorming. At the time, there were hundreds of groups and it seemed every time we thought of a name someone was there before us. We eventually came up with The Quandowns. This had no meaning at all but George was good at art and came up with a drawing of a vampire like character that was painted on to the front of my bass drum. This was to become the mythical Quandown.

It was decided that the youth club would hold a dance and we would provide the live entertainment. It was 1962 and this was to be our first proper gig. I don't recall having any nerves, as we all felt ready and confident in each other. I was finding it a little awkward without a high hat as my foot was stuck out of the side of the kit with nothing to work. This made playing the bass drum difficult as one balanced the other. I was hoping that with the fee we would get from our performance, I could invest in one as soon as possible. The other missing item for me was a floor tom tom and just to make matters worse, we had added Tommy Roe's 'Sheila' as one of our vocal numbers. The drum track on this record is entirely floor tom tom. The small tom tom I had was tuned too high for the purpose, so I had to stand up and play the part on the front head of the bass drum. It was painful leaning over the drum for the whole number and of course, when a band learned a new number, they wanted to play it several times a night. This was managed by mystery requests on various pieces of paper appearing in Bob's hand. We, of course, had written the requests earlier.

I also discovered to my horror that the head on the bass drum was the old fashioned vellum and not the plastic heads that were more commonly used at the time. This was fine at first but as the evening progressed and the room began to heat up, the skin began to stretch and instead of a lovely deep boom sound the bass drum would be making a 'boink' like sound which was not good at all. I used to slacken off all the tension keys until they were completely loose but the 'boink' was still there! It was obvious that I needed some sorting out if we were going to do regular gigs. Investments were being made by all the boys as time went by and George acquired a white Fender Stratocaster, Bob a Watkins Rapier (left handed) and an echo chamber.

At first we were playing only at the Youth Club and community halls in the area that ran dances. Then we got a regular booking at a dance that was held in the hall of Farringdon School not far from where we lived. It had a big stage and proper lights and built up to be a very popular Saturday night dance. Thankfully with these few gigs I was able to buy a Premier Floor Tom Tom and a hi-hat. At least now I had a full kit. We had also, by necessity acquired a van. None of us could drive so we used various friends who were happy to make a little money and enjoy the gig. It was an old post office van which had been converted and even had curtains in the windows. We set about 'decorating' the van with lipstick graffiti so that we looked more popular than we actually were. Needless to say we each wrote 'We love John' or We love Bob' until there was not a square inch not covered.

We were building a good reputation in and around Sunderland, and even though we were under age, started to play pubs and the working men's clubs throughout the area. In the 1960's, Sunderland boasted over two hundred working men's clubs which provided entertainment seven nights a week. It is hard to imagine now, but for a cover charge of as little as a shilling (10p now) you could see a group and a singer or comedian most nights and a game of bingo in the middle! All the clubs were run as non-profit organisations and they even had their own Federation brewery so the drinks were cheap as well.

On stage at Farringdon School Dance, Sunderland (circa 1963)

This provided a wealth of work for the groups that were springing up all over the place to fulfil the demand. Opposite Ewesley Road Youth Club was St. Gabriel's, which was Church of England and they also had their own youth club. They also had their own resident group in competition to us called The Fireflies. Two of the members of this band were a youthful Nigel Olsen on drums and Mick Grabham on guitar. Mick and I were mates, as we had gone to Monkwearmouth College of Further Education and used to share the Number 18 bus home each day. Whenever either of us was on a break, we would sneak across the road to check out what songs they were playing and how many people were in their club. It was a sign of the times that such was the interest in live music that both clubs would be packed out every Friday night. Luck was to come to Nigel and Mick, when a chance meeting with a singer called Brian Keith at the Seaburn Hall gave them their break. Brian had recorded a song called 'Everything I Am' which was doing well under the name Plastic Penny and he need a group. They went off to London and the record was a hit. Sitting watching them on Top of the Pops made us envious and we wondered if luck would eventually shine on us. Nigel went on the work with Elton John and Mick played guitar with several bands including Cochise and Procol Harum.

Things were moving apace with regular bookings coming in all the time. Around this time Clive decided to leave the band as his heart was not in it. He had just wanted it to be a hobby and it was all moving a bit too fast for him. From just playing a Friday night at the youth club, we were now pulling in around 5 dates a week. I knew a bass player called Peter Watson and he was a talented musician. His father was also a bass player who played in bands so he came from a good solid musical background. Peter came and sat in on a rehearsal and fitted in straight away. He had a good sense of humour and we got on really well as we shared a love of scooters.

Early publicity shot for The Quandowns (L/R Bob, Pete, John & Ron Madison)

Many times Peter and I would ride through to Newcastle on our Lambretta scooters to visit the music shops there. We would try out the Fenders and Gibson guitars and I would look longingly at the new drum kits. I remember once driving onto the forecourt of a petrol station before one of these visits. I asked the attendant (no self service in those days) for half a gallon of 2 star petrol. In true Northern style humour he said to me 'Half a gallon of 2 star bonny lad, you must be off to Europe then?' With Peter in the band and finally settled, we all descended on Burtons the Tailor in the High Street in town to get suits made especially for stage. Presentation was very much a part of groups then and with acts like Cliff and the Shadows and the Mersey beat bands, you had to have proper stage wear to be taken seriously. After looking at various outfits, the one we settled for was a charcoal grey shiny suit with black piping round the jacket.

It was around this time that I decided I needed to up grade the kit. What had started out as a bit of fun was now developing at pace. We were doing a lot of gigs and certainly getting a good local reputation. Following some of the scooter journeys to Newcastle, I had my heart set on a Ludwig super classic kit. My favourite instrument store was Max Share's Music Shop, as I had seen just the kit I wanted. It was in grey oyster pearl and looked magnificent. So was the price! The price of the kit was £299 guineas. For those who can't remember, a guinea was £1 and one shilling and in 1964 this was a lot of money. I waited for the moment to discuss this with my mother. She went slightly white when I mentioned the price. After much thought, she declared that she would sign the hire purchase agreement only if I got a proper job. So the quest was on to get that sorted.

I scanned the Sunderland Echo each evening and spotted an advert for an 'office boy' at Vaux Breweries. They were one of the biggest breweries in the North East and run by the Nicholson family, who had a big military history. I hand wrote my application and sent it off to the company secretary in due course. A few days later I got a reply asking me to go for an interview. All donned up in my suit, shirt and tie, not to mention polished shoes, I set off for the brewery in the town centre. The interview went well and I was told 290 boys had applied for the job. Unbelievably, I was offered the job. My starting salary was about £4 a week. I was making around £20 a week from gigs so this was only a means to get the Ludwig drum kit. I started two weeks later in the general office.

The duties were very menial and there was a lot of licking of envelopes and dog's body stuff. One job I had was to sort and distribute the post when it came in, for every department. In a brewery there are a lot but one in particular held dread for us all. The stables! They got one letter a month which was the invoice for the hay. Vaux had several magnificent dray horses which pulled the carts that they used for the town based pubs. The stable boys were pretty rough and considered us 'suits' as complete puffs. No matter how hard we tried, when it came to delivering the monthly letter, we could never get in and out of the stables without a kicking.

Mum, true to her word, now signed on the dotted line for the new drums. She had arranged to go through to Newcastle one afternoon with our driver to collect them. I couldn't wait to finish at Vaux that afternoon. As soon as the clock hit 5pm, I was off down the stairs, kick started the Lambrettor and off up Hylton Road to home as fast as the machine could take me.

When I got there, the kit was parked in the front room. I just sat on the sofa and stared at it. It was absolutely beautiful and I couldn't believe it was mine. I gave Mum a huge hug and thanked her for once again helping me out. I did not have much time to admire it, as we had a gig that night at the Shildon Railway Institute. They ran a weekly dance on a Wednesday night and it was well attended by all the local kids. I had not told the band I was getting the new kit, as I wanted to be sure I had got it before telling them. When the van turned up at my house, the roadie jumped out of the van and up the path to collect the kit. By this time the drums were in their black cases, but he could tell they were new. Everyone was well chuffed when I told them and couldn't wait for the gig to try them out.

It was with huge pride that I set them up when we got to the gig. One thing I hadn't considered was how different they would feel to the old drums. The main difference was the size of the bass drum. The Ludwig drum was 22" and so much larger than the old Beverley. It was like sitting on top of mountain in comparison. However, after a couple of numbers it was no problem and it certainly sounded twice as loud as the old lot. It added so much to the look of the group and we were all well pleased. Shortly after my purchase, Bob got the bug and bought a Vox twelve string guitar which had featured on the Hollies' hit 'I'm Alive'.

We were now playing at the Top Rank Suite, Club 11 in Villiers Street, The Bay Hotel and The Locarno Ballroom in Sunderland which were major gigs in the area. There was also a really good club in the town centre called the El Cubana. Situated in Toward Road close to Mowbray Park, it was a four storey house that also had a cellar. The El Cubana was a coffee club and eventually, the owner Eric Punshon, managed to get a liquor license. He then also opened La Cubana so the two clubs ran side by side on different floors. They would often have two groups playing there. One would play on the first floor and the other would play in the basement. The atmosphere was electric with so many people rammed into a confined space. The good thing was that the groups and the public could get up close and personal to each other and each seemed to bounce off the other with their enthusiasm. The club pulled off a coup when they booked The Spencer Davies Group just before they charted with their first hit 'Keep on Runnin'. You can imagine the queue to get in that night was half way round the town centre. It was a fantastic night, great atmosphere and packed to the brim. Seeing a group like that up close made us more determined than ever to keep going and improve. Eric became a legend in the North East with the groups and he was always very fair with us all – and we always got paid! Liverpool historically has always got the acclaim for clubs like The Cavern because of their association with The Beatles. However, the club scene in Sunderland and Newcastle was very vibrant and there were probably more clubs in the area than Liverpool at the time.

The dance floor at the La Cubana in Sunderland. (Note the chic 60's furniture)

One of the regulars at the La Cubana was a guy called John Briggs who, with his mates from Southmoor School, would be there every weekend. On one of these nights around Christmas time, his mates put some sugar cubes in his drinks. This of course accelerated the alcohol intake into his blood stream and he got very drunk. As soon as he left the hot club, the cold air hit him like a train and made him ill. He felt so bad that he ended up on his hands and knees, crawling the entire length of Toward Road. Somehow he managed to get on to Ryhope Road, a major road out of Sunderland towards his home.

As he was almost home, he suddenly heard a voice say 'Are we enjoying ourselves then?' Looking up from the pavement, there was a police officer looking at him from the window of a passing patrol car. Asking where he lived, John did some quick thinking and just pointed at the house he was in front of. Told to get inside by the police before he was arrested for being drunk and disorderly, he staggered through the gate and made his way to the front door. Thankfully the police drove off and he was able to make it to his own house where it took several days to recover. The other casualty was his suit, which now had no knees in the trousers and his mother had to cash in her Co-op 'divi' to get a new one.

Life in the Quandowns continued, but there was tension building in the band with George. Up until now, from the formation of the band, we had all been together as mates and nothing had interfered with rehearsals or our live work. However, George had started to go out with a girl who would be brought along to every rehearsal and gig and would never leave George's side. She was, in hindsight, the original Yoko Ono. It did not sit well with us and none of us liked the situation. She would even chip in with comments on what songs we should be learning and making comments on how we played. To make matters even worse, she had a sister who was the size of a house. George insisted on bringing his girlfriend and this sister to every gig. They all travelled in the van with us and it meant members of the band having to sit on amplifiers in the back of the van as the seats were all taken up by this motley crew. The sister also had serious body odour problems and in the summer, it became unbearable. The atmosphere in the band to this situation was becoming positively hostile. It got to the stage where we could not take it any longer.

We dreaded the next gig and seeing the van pull up in front of the house with that lot occupying all the seats was a revolution waiting to happen. We agreed to meet without George and it was decided he had to go. This was not going to be easy, as he was a very volatile character and liable to lose it at any given time. Frankly, we were scared of him and his temper and that was one of the reasons we had put up with the situation for so long. It was left to Bob to tell him he was fired. This was because Bob was his closest friend and it was felt he was the only one who could give him the news without being beaten to a pulp. The next day Bob went round to see George and told him the news. George was furious and after some unpleasant shouting, the door was firmly slammed in Bob's face.

We had already put out some feelers for a new guitarist. At first we got in Bob's girl friend's brother, Dennis Whitfield but he didn't last very long as his guitar playing was not much better than mine! Eventually, the guy that fitted the bill was a local guitarist called Ron Maddison. Technically, he was not that great, but could play all the songs we had in our repertoire. He was a lovely lad, tall and good looking and more importantly – no girlfriend! He played a Gibson 303 and had a good amplifier and microphone. Within days he was slotted in to the band as well and we were back up and running with a diary full of dates. The atmosphere changed instantly and again we looked forward to playing and doing gigs. It showed just how corrosive the situation had become with George and we were all back to being a unit once more.

Chapter Five

The El Cubana became a regular date for us, playing as well as just hanging out when we were not playing and watching other bands. It also attracted all sorts of people interested in the local music scene at the time. It was on one of our dates there that we were introduced to a manager called Geoff Hibberd. Up until then, we had managed all our own bookings through agents and I had taken charge of that area of the band. He certainly had a good tale to tell. He also mentioned he had friends, Colin Pearson and John Wray, who were agents booking bands for clubs in Germany. This impressed us a great deal and we were all ears. I guess we were seduced by the temptation of the big time or at least the chance to travel abroad which appealed to us a lot. We had heard about the German clubs and it seemed a good move. Auditions were being set up by the agents at the El Cubana one afternoon and we were duly invited. We arrived and set up on the first floor. It was out first audition as all our previous work had come from recommendations.

Seeing all the other bands setting up and then watching us perform was quite intimidating. We did our spot and started to pack the gear away and back into the van. Geoff came to see us and said the agents were impressed but the club they had in mind really wanted a girl singer. Did we know anyone? It all seemed to be going wrong now as we were so confident. Then, as the reality of the situation became more apparent, Ron our guitarist who was due to be getting married wanted out if we were going to Germany. Bob and I were distraught as we felt our big chance was slipping away. We were so set on going as we saw this as our chance to get the break we so desired.

Not only finding a guitarist, but someone committed enough to go to Germany was proving difficult. Bob knew a keyboard player called Malcolm Wright who lived in Hartlepool. We hadn't considered a keyboard player before now. When he told us he was also going out with a girl called Marie Greaser who he said he could persuade to sing a few numbers, we thought we had solved the problem. Bob would take the role of lead guitar from Ron and Malcolm would come in on organ with Marie providing a few songs to satisfy the German club. We set up some rehearsals and deep down we weren't at all happy. Malcolm was not that great a player and his girlfriend was not a very good singer. A fine pair. She learnt 'These Boots Are Made for Walking' together with a few more songs and we auditioned again for the agents. We went through the same repertoire and then introduced Marie. We only got her to do the one song, 'Boot's' so as not to overexpose her. Somehow they accepted us and offered us our first engagement. They said we would be required to do a month first off and gave us the details. It was to be at the Funny Crow Club situated in Grindelberg. It was in a suburb of Hamburg just a few short miles from the Reeperbahn.

I then had to resign from Vaux. It was just nine months since they had employed me and I had to go back to the company secretary's office to explain why I was leaving so soon. When I explained the chance that I had to go to Germany, he looked at me as if I was completely mad. To be fair, he wished me well and I returned to my office hoping that I had made the right decision. It did not go unnoticed at home that the reason for my Mum signing for the drums was just about to disappear. She must have realised just how much this opportunity meant to me and again she backed me to follow my dream.

It was April 1966 and we were rehearsing frantically for the trip to Germany. Marie was not making much progress in the vocal section and we were only going to use her sparingly during each night. It was going to put a lot of pressure on Bob vocal wise, as the hours we were due to play were far beyond the two forty five minute sets we had been used to. We had to drive to Liverpool one day to get our passports as this was the nearest office to us where we could get them while we waited. It was a terrible drive in bad weather, all stuck in the back of the van and Liverpool in the rain seemed to be hell on earth.

Geoff was now driving for us as none of us had a license, so we were quite dependent on him. After a long wait in the queue, we were given our new dark blue passports boldly proclaiming 'Her Britannic Majesty's principal secretary of State requests...' Surely with this kind of recommendation, nothing could stop us going to Germany now. We made it back to Sunderland late in the evening and two days later, packed and ready to go, it was time.

The van was loaded to the hilt with gear and we had got a new Vox PA, on advice from Geoff, from Saville's music store in Holmeside in Sunderland. Bob's mum had signed for it on hire purchase and the band would pay the instalments from our money in Germany. In 1966, vans and cars were still very basic, not least a ten year old Austin A4 van. Radios were extras as were heaters and guess what? Our van didn't have a heater or a radio. Entertainment was provided by a small portable radio hung from the driver's door. Heat in the van was provided by large amounts of clothing worn by every occupant and the only seating was the driver and passenger. Those who drew the short straw had to sit on drum cases and amps in the back which was agony.

As the van drew up outside my house, I said my goodbyes to my mum who looked on with anxious anticipation and a look that said 'What have I let you into now!' It was the 28th April 1966 and the journey to Dover was long and tedious. With little or no motorways, just the old A1, we chugged south and Hamburg seemed light years away.

At the port of Dover, it was a sight to behold. Talk about an Exodus! The car park was full of group vans all making their way to Europe to work. It was quite remarkable the state of the vehicles, considering the journeys they were about to undertake. Some bands we talked to were driving to Italy and Spain and there was more rust than steel on their vans. We bought our tickets and gently drove on to the ferry, hoping it wouldn't break down while driving on. We knew they would not allow any vehicle aboard that was not driveable. So far, so good. The crossing was uneventful and it was good to get some sea air in the lungs. Seeing the White Cliffs of Dover disappear on the horizon is a very poignant moment for anyone British and the first pangs of homesickness began to sink in. The realisation that we were off to a foreign country sunk in. Having never been away from home for any amount of time before, made me feel very apprehensive. At least we all had each other to help out, which was something.

We made our way from Oostende to Antwerp, where we stopped to have a meal. It was all new territory ordering foreign food and most of us ended up with egg and chips. We soon discovered that bread in Europe was not the nice soft sliced Hovis we had been used to and tea was served in a hot cup of water with a tea bag by the side. Postcards were written, posted and we started on the long drive up the autobahns crossing into Germany at Venlo where we handed over our nice shiny new passports and then headed north towards Hamburg. We drove into Hamburg the following morning; it was raining and it made the city look dour and imposing. It was hard not to imagine we were in an army truck entering into Hamburg as the allied troops had done only twenty years earlier. The Funny Crow Club was in the Hamburg suburb of Grindelberg, about a ten minute drive from the Reeperbahn. The club had arranged for us to stay in a bed and breakfast establishment a short distance from the club.

Following a very rough map we eventually found the street it was in. It was a large four storey building and the front door housed many door bells with strange names attached to each. After some trial and error we found the right one and were escorted up to our rooms. There was a large room for the boys and one for Marie. It was dark, damp and horrible. The view from our bedroom window was the adjoining wall of the next building. It did not escape our notice that there were pock marks in the wall that looked suspiciously like large bullet holes. Obviously the effects of the Second World War had not been completely obliterated. We unpacked our suitcases from the van and set off to find the club. It was situated in a large shopping parade and looked quite good from the outside. We checked out the area and found a cheap place to eat.

Chapter Six

The club opened around 2pm for cleaning and deliveries and we were able to get in and set up our gear. The stage was two tiered, so I set up on the top tier at the back with Bob, Malcolm and Peter in the front. Marie would find a spot in between to sing her few numbers when asked. The club owner was an Israeli called Alexander Zuker. He was a nice man and made us feel very welcome. We were very excited about playing and had a good sound check. Geoff had disappeared while we were sound checking and we didn't think anything of it at the time. We decided to go back to the digs to get cleaned up and changed but no Geoff. We had to walk back to the digs as our transport had disappeared and after some wrong turns eventually found the place. Still no Geoff, so we had to also walk back to the club as we were due to do our first set at 7pm. When we got back he was there and told us he had just gone for a look around town in the van.

We started playing and there was a good crowd at the start, building as the night went on. We went down really well and I think we played just the kind of pop that the crowd wanted to hear. Marie did her few numbers but I noticed Alexander and his manager at the bar looking in the direction of the stage with strange expressions on their faces every time she sang. They were long nights and at the Funny Crow we played forty minutes on and twenty minutes off, playing through until 2am each day. In Germany at that time, people under the age of 18 could go into clubs until 10pm. I was given the job of having to read out this paragraph in German basically telling anyone under 18 they had to leave the club.

On stage at The Funny Crow Club, Hamburg 1966

The club population in Hamburg in those days was a very itinerant group of people and they would go from one club to another. There was the Star Club and Top Ten Club on or near the Reeperbahn, The Big Apple and Funny Crow on the outskirts and the result was always a good and responsive crowd on the dance floor. If someone in the audience requested a tune and you played it, a waiter would bring a tray of scotch and coke for the band from the grateful punters. This was something new for us, as in the past we had generally only got given abuse for not playing a song that someone felt they had some God given right to ask for.

As the night drew on, a waiter was bringing a regular tray of scotch and cokes for me and leaving them by the side of my kit. At the next break I asked him who was buying these for me. He pointed to a blond girl sitting at the bar and I wandered over to thank her for the drinks. We got talking and as I was leaving to play the next set, she asked me if I would go back to her place when we had finished. I nearly fainted. In Sunderland at that time, you were lucky if you got to hold a girl's hand and have a quick snog. Within twenty four hours of leaving my Methodist home and upbringing, I was in Hamburg and being asked to spend the night with a German girl.

I relayed this to the boys and they were making the most of it, winding me up and I felt more terrified by their behaviour than hers. At the next break I found out her name was Renate and she lived relatively close by. I decided to make my excuses as I wanted to bottle out. This was all too soon for me. I hadn't even spent a night in the digs yet. She was having none of it and was quite forceful. The night ended and the boys set off for their digs and I waved them goodbye as our taxi headed off into the unknown with someone I had only met a few hours before. I was quaking in my shoes when we got to her apartment. Here we were, naked in bed and she was all over me. She even provided the condom and without romance or love, my virginity was gone forever. I laid in her bed and felt a mix of emotion. It was exhilarating and scary at the same time. I had only been in Germany one night and done what I had not had the bottle to do back home. I wanted to be with the boys as they were family in this adventure somehow I felt I had deserted them. Eventually, I sank into a deep sleep as the journey and a hard night on stage had taken their toll.

Her alarm shattered the stillness of the room the next morning and I was rolled out of bed, dressed and out the door as she went off to work. She pointed to a bus and told me which one to board to get back to the Funny Crow. I might as well have been left on the moon. I just about managed to find my way back to the Funny Crow with all these German commuters and from there, walked to the digs. It was around 7am and I made my way up to our room ready to collapse into my own bed for the rest of the day. Malcolm, having Marie in tow, was well supplied with condoms. The boys had filled one of these with condensed milk, tied a knot in it and put it in my bed. As I climbed in under the duvet I slid over this monstrosity. I was still tired and all I wanted to do was sleep. I picked the horrible thing up, walked over to the window and threw it out of the window. That was my first mistake of the tour. I watched as the offending condom sailed down through the air, its journey almost frozen in time. It hit the washing line in the yard below and neatly wrapped itself around the line, finally hanging limp with the offending condensed milk swinging gently in the breeze. It just so happened that the landlady was hanging out her washing at the time of this unfortunate occurrence and she stared in horror at the offending item. She looked up towards our window and the look on her face was like thunder. Whatever we said to try and appease her, she was having none of it and it was quite clear she wanted us out of there. We had watched too many war films not to know what 'Raus' meant. Geoff, having looked at the digs had said he was checking into a hotel in the city, which he would pay for himself. When he came to collect us that morning we were sitting on the pavement on our cases looking very forlorn; especially me.

The consequences of this eviction were to be financial more than anything else. There were not too many places in Hamburg in 1966 that were keen to accommodate English musicians. We had to decamp to the Hotel Willy Pfeifer in Hallerstrasse, almost opposite the club. It was far superior to our previous hostelry but it came at a price. We had worked out a budget which would have left us nicely off at the end of the month and now our hotel budget had doubled! The following night Renate was waiting and with the events of that morning, I had mentally moved on. Unfortunately Renate had not. I tried to keep a low profile all night but she was not to be moved. At the end of the evening, I was out of the club being chased by this mad German woman who now thought she owned me! After all, it was her that chatted me up and not the other way around so I didn't have any feeling of guilt. Thankfully I could run faster than her and managed to evade her for at least one night. She stood there crying and screaming in the middle of the road as we made our way back to the hotel for some peace and quiet. Wow, we had only been here forty-eight hours!

While we were sitting around during the day, Geoff suggested we do some publicity stunt to get our name in the papers. That way we could attract a wider interest in the band and get more work. So far, we only had the first month at The Funny Crow followed by a month at a new club called The Ambassadeur in a town called Bad Salzuflen which was near Bielefeld. After some crazy ideas, it was decided that we would jump into Lake Alster fully clothed. This was a huge lake in the centre of Hamburg and regularly had boats sailing around it's perimeter with lots of tourists. It was decided that we would launch ourselves from one of the quays where the boats left from. We got some friends to speak to a few of the Hamburg papers who were interested in English bands at the time and this seemed like something that captured their imagination. Four crazy English musicians willing to drown themselves for a story had to warrant a few column inches. Photographers were lined up and we duly made our way to the designated spot.

The quay was opposite where the British Embassy was located with its spectacular view across the lake. The quay was busy with tourists and they were curious when they saw us all standing on top of the railings. With the photographers in place, we waited for the signal and jumped. It was bloody freezing and we seemed to go down very deep. I felt the rush of cold water go past my face and start to invade all the clothes I was wearing. After what seemed like an eternity, I broke the surface and looked round to see Peter and Malcolm but no Bob. We looked around frantically and I saw his face deep in the water looking up. It looked as white as a sheet. I was just about to dive down when suddenly he started to rise and surfaced. He was coughing up water and looked very scared. We climbed up the railings with difficulty and lay out on the quay exhausted. It occurred to us how close we had come to loosing Bob and no one had thought to put any safety measures in place.

Outside the British Embassy in Hamburg 1966 after jumping in the Lake Alster for a publicity stunt
(L/R John, Pete, Bob & Malcolm)

It was a scary moment and we hoped that the resulting press coverage would be worth it. We staggered across the road and laid out on the lawns of the Embassy. In those days, before terrorism had raised its ugly head, security was a lot more relaxed and no one bothered us. Thankfully, it was a sunny day and we could dry off and take in the sun. The photographers were happy with the shots they had got and said they would get them off to the papers as soon as they were developed. Remarkably several of the papers carried the story the following day and when we turned up at the Funny Crow that night, quite a few of the locals had copies of the paper with us in it.

HERZLICHE GRÜSSE VON DEN „QUANDOWNS", NORD-ENGLANDS SPITZEN-
BEAT-GRUPPE, AUF TOURNEE IN DEUTSCHLAND.

JOHN   BOB   PETER   MAC COLM

THE GEOFF HIBBERD ORGANISATION, LONDON

One of the publicity handouts printed for us by Coca-Cola International. This is us walking back to our van after jumping in Lake Alster fully clothed. The photo got the names wrong as L/R – Malcolm, Bob, John and Pete. In the back ground is our legendary German road manager Arnde Weydemeyer (In suit shirt and tie on right). He was to save our lives some months later.

Despite being in the papers, by the end of the week with our finances in tatters, we were not able to eat very much as most of our money was going on the hotel. One night Alexander approached us and asked if we were OK? We explained what had happened and he was very surprised we were short of money. We said that due to the hotel being more expensive it was hitting out budget and we didn't want to end up with no money at the end of the month. He took us down to his office and showed us a ledger which detailed all the money that had been taken out of our month's money. All the signatures were Geoff's and he had taken almost all our money out and we had only been there two weeks. Alexander was suspicious of Geoff and it proved a defining moment. We were horrified and furious at the same time.

While we were starving and playing eight hours a night, he was off living it up on our money. It was now that we discovered he had a thing for boys. How naïve had we been? No wonder he wanted a hotel somewhere different from us. Shortly before the club opened that night, he came in for his usual visit before disappearing into the night in search of male company. Malcolm being the biggest of us all was the first to confront Geoff as he came through the door. Foolishly, when confronted with his misdeeds he threatened to walk out and take Malcolm's passport, which for some reason he still had. Malcolm grabbed Geoff by his jacket and we thought Malcolm was going to kill him. In his terror, Geoff dropped the passport and us at the same time. He was out of the door and gone. So, after just two weeks in Hamburg, we had spent most of our month's money, we were staying in a hotel twice as expensive as we could afford and now our manager had gone and worse still, taken the van. World travelled teenagers would be hard pressed to understand our naivety but this was 1966 and we were as green as grass when it came to homosexuality. Now, we had no transport and none of us could drive even if he had left the van. Up 'shit creak without a paddle' was about where we were at that moment in time.

As if things couldn't get any worse, Alexander came to see us and said he didn't want Marie to sing any longer. It was sad for her, as she had only tried to help and even though she didn't want to leave Malcolm, it came as some relief for all concerned. So, her music career was over and her parents arranged for her to fly home. I think she realised that she would never get Malcolm back and he was about to set out on a mission to bed as many German girls as he could. Something he managed to do with great success. Thankfully, Alexander liked us and we were doing good business for his club as it was now full every night. We had made some good friends in the club and our popularity was spreading. One of our new German friends was a big guy called Arnde Weydemeyer. He loved the group and lived with his parents in Grindelberg. He seemed to be at a loose end and didn't have a job. We explained what had happened with Geoff and he offered to help us. He also had a valid driving licence.

Chapter Seven

One of the directors of the Funny Crow was opening a new club called The Ambassadeur in Bielefeld and had booked us to open the club the following month. The only problem was now we had no means of getting there as Geoff had legged it back to England with the van. Arnde had heard that Coca-Cola had sponsored some groups recently and maybe they could help. It was a wild notion, but we had nothing to lose. We found the telephone number of Coco-Cola International in the phone book and after some persuasion and a lot of bullshit, about how we were the greatest living band on the planet; we managed to get a meeting with the marketing director.

The following day we set off for the German HQ of Coca-Cola International in Hamburg and waited in the grand reception for our meeting. Arnde had come with us for support and to help us find our way around the Hamburg public transport system. We were finally shown in to the office. The guy was young and very into English bands. We liked him a lot and we all got on very well. He listened to our predicament and sat back in his chair scratching his head. 'Well' he said, 'I can't give you a van, but I can arrange for our drivers to take you and your equipment to your next booking in Bad Salzuflen'. He had a problem, as this was outside his sales area. He made a couple of calls, checked the date we needed the transport and we were sorted. A van would pick us up at 9am on the morning we were due to leave and take us half way. It would rendezvous with another Coca Cola van on the autobahn from the next district and they would take us on to Bad Salzuflen. He also arranged to have several thousand give away photo cards from the photo shoot of the Lake Alster stunt. He had seen it in the papers and was impressed with our promotion. We left his office feeling elated and for four Northern boys from Sunderland, we felt we had grown up a lot in two weeks.

Arnde was getting ever closer to us and we asked him if he was interested in being our roadie? He jumped at the chance and would make the journey to Bad Salzuflen with us. The owner of the Ambassadeur Club there said he would advance us some of our month's money so we could purchase a van when we got there. Another bonus for us at the next club was that as it was a converted cinema, it had lots of room and part of the upstairs had been converted into accommodation for the bands, so no expensive hotel bills or stroppy Fraus to throw us all out!

We now played the remaining two weeks at the Funny Crow with renewed enthusiasm. A great weight had lifted off our shoulders and we could relax at least for a while. The hours we were playing were long and starting to take their toll on our voices. It has been described by many musicians as 'The Hamburg Throat'. Singing for hours in smoky conditions for around six to eight hours a night, when we were used to doing only two forty-five minute sets at home was hard. The bonus was however, that once we got through the pain barrier, the harmonies and vocals became tighter.

We had practised most afternoons, once we had had a good sleep, to increase our repertoire. This was to keep the crowds enthused with new tunes from the current chart, but also to stimulate us, as it got tedious playing the same 30 tunes each night. Bob had a portable record player and we would buy singles of the latest releases. They were basically released almost simultaneously with the UK. In Germany, the singles were packaged much more attractively than the UK, as instead of the paper house bag from Decca or Columbia, they would have a photograph of the artist on the sleeve. In Hamburg at that time, the club audiences were amazingly transient. Each club used to stamp the punter's hands and give them a 'pass out' and they would spend a couple of hours in one club and then go off to another and so on. I have never encountered anything quite like Hamburg in the 60s. Its nightlife was unique to any other city in the world I have ever visited. There were clubs there which bragged that during World War 2 'We never closed' and I can believe it. Looking back now, it is hard to believe the people who frequented these clubs lived a normal life during the day and went to their offices or jobs. They got to see loads of bands each evening and we didn't have to entertain the same crowd all night. It worked very well, although it was hard as the dawn approached and the dance floor was still full of enthusiastic revellers.

It felt strange to be leaving the Funny Crow, as we had made a lot of friends there. We had done good business for the club and Alexander was very happy with us. He wanted to book us again and it was agreed we would return in two months time. When we looked back, the events that had taken place over the previous four weeks had been extraordinary. Driving a thousand miles to Hamburg to a country that was as alien as Mars was to us. Been thrown out of our accommodation after only one night, losing my virginity, finding out our manager had embezzled us, left in Hamburg with no transport and none of us could drive. Surely it could only get better from here on in?

The Sunday morning arrived after playing a storming last set before saying our good byes to the Funny Crow crowd. The manager was there to open the club, so we could get our gear out and into the Coca Cola van for our ride to Bad Salzuflen. As we left the outskirts of Hamburg, we all still felt vulnerable and alone. Even if we now had Arnde who spoke the language, we knew we had a fair amount of catching up to do. The journey was uneventful and we were silent in our thoughts as we turned off the Autobahn to meet up with the other van that would take us the final stage of the journey. We off loaded all the gear and onto the other van which was identical to the first one, a lovely shiny new Mercedes with the Coca Cola logo all over it. If only we could keep it! The driver was keen to get us on our way so we had no time for refreshments. After an hour we were following the signs to Bielefeld and then on to Bad Salzuflen. It was a small town and a lot different to the cosmopolitan feel of Hamburg. The club was close to the town centre at least, so we wouldn't have far to check out the local hostelries.

The club owner and his wife were nice and made us feel very welcome. The club itself was not opening for a few days after we arrived, so there was not too much panic about getting the gear up. We thanked the driver for his help and after quick handshakes, he was gone. We were here but no transport. We were shown up to our rooms which although not plush, were clean and comfortable and warm. We had our own entrance round the back of the club which Malcolm eyed with a glint in his eye. Since the tearful departure of his girlfriend Marie, Malcolm had begun a mission to bed as many fräuleins as he possibly could. So far, his mission could be said to be extremely successful judging by the nightly traffic to and from his bed. Added to this, he had taken to collecting a photograph of each of them and the portfolio was so large he could hardly get the lid of his suitcase closed. We were no angels, and were entertaining the girls when and if we found someone we liked, but Malcolm's Olympian mission continued with immense dedication.

As we had arrived early evening and we hadn't had a chance to buy any food, we decided to go check out the place and find somewhere to have something to eat and drink. After a quick wash and change of clothes, we left the club and headed into downtown Bad Salzuflen. The first bier haus seemed OK with lots of locals and a good atmosphere and in we went. It was like a scene from an old Wild West movie. The music stopped, the locals stopped talking and the barman stopped polishing the glass in his hand as he glared at us. This was very strange to us as the young people in Hamburg could not have been friendlier. Before we could say 'Four Pints and a packet of crisps' the barman was shouting 'Raus', 'Raus' at us and Arnde had a look of total disbelief on his face. We had read enough war comics to know that we weren't exactly being welcomed with open arms and turned on our heels and were back on the street ready to run. I half expected the barman to shout 'Hande Hoch' and 'Donner und Blitzen' before we could leave to bar.

I said, 'I don't know about you lads, but fuck this for a lark, this lot look like they would be happy to see us shot against a wall than serve us a pint of lager'. Arnde was also shocked and hadn't experienced anything like it either. That said, he hadn't ventured much further than Hamburg and this was a little out in the sticks by comparison. We all felt that we must have just picked the wrong place with a crowd not too keen on the English. It was 1966 and the Second World War was still ripe in the older people's minds. The next place we encountered we approached with much more caution. We sent in Arnde ahead of us this time to check out the place. He beckoned us in, but as soon as the locals heard us speak English, the familiar hostility was all too apparent and we were off before we were carted off to Stalag Luft 13. This was not looking good and if this was a taster for the month ahead, I for one as not exactly looking forward to the experience. We had, by now, done an almost complete circle of the town and we had one more place to try before returning to the club totally rejected, hungry and not least very thirsty! The last place we tried was situated on Rudolf-Brandes Allee called 'Onkel Paul's' and this time we said that Arnde had to go in and speak to the owner and ask if we would be welcome. Sooner or later, we felt that it could turn nasty enough for us to get attacked, it was that bad.

Arnde duly pushed through the doors of Onkel Paul's and disappeared into the depths of its darkened interior. By now, we were anxious, cold and hungry and were wondering where our next food was going to come from. After ten long lonely minutes Arnde appeared onto the street. We were all searching his face for the slightest hint of emotion that would tell whether we were in or out. Slowly a glint of a smile came on his face and he told us 'We're in boys, the owner is a young man from Hamburg and we are all welcome'.

His name was Erich Volkmann and he was our saviour for the month. I can't tell you how much of a collective relief we all felt.

We still entered the place nervously but we were immediately put at ease by a big cheery smile from behind the bar. Well, it was pilsners all round and to toast the welcome relief of finding a friendly place, we all had schnapps chasers to boot. We tucked into Bratwurst and pommes frites and the banter was good. So good in fact that the rounds were mounting at an alarming rate. During the evening, Erich came and joined us as another round of foaming pilsners and schnapps arrived at the table. We asked Erich why everyone in the town was so against us. With some nonchalance, Erich explained that during the War, Bad Salzuflen had been a Gestapo Headquarters, and he said that many of the people in the town were still very bitter about the War and hated the English. There was, of course, a massive army presence in the area near Bielefeld as a constant reminder to them of their defeat. This was something that had passed us by in Hamburg, as we had mostly been with the younger German teenagers who didn't have the same issues. We all raised a toast to Erich and Onkel Paul's and thanked him for his kindness.

Ten pilsners and schnapps chasers later, we were completely pissed. After the travelling, lack of food and then the relief of finding a friendly place, we had been consumed by the events of the day. Now the tricky bit was not only getting back to the Ambassadeur Club, but finding it and getting back inside. Arnde was the most capable and managed to escort Malcolm, Bob and Pete back to the club. They were confronted by two German policemen on the way back and very nearly thrown into the cells with a whack from a baton for good measure. Arnde's negotiating skills in tricky circumstances were certainly coming in handy, as he managed to persuade them to let them go on their way. Somehow, I got lost from the pack and stumbled around the streets looking for a familiar sign. Frankly, if I had walked into the front doors of the club I wouldn't have recognised it! Panic and paranoia set in now as the memory of the hostile locals started to flood back to my mind.

I had visions of a blood thirsty pack of Germans with big dogs chasing me through the town and making sure I never got behind my drum kit ever again. I didn't have a rank and number I could quote. 'For you Tommy, the War is over'. That seemed funny in war films, sitting on the back seat of the Regal Cinema in Pallion, Sunderland tucking into a quarter of Midget Gems. It wasn't bloody funny falling around pissed in the middle of a town that still regarded the Gestapo with affection. In the darkness, the last thing I remember was finding some thick bushes and pushing my way into the depths of their foliage to hide from the enemy. I slipped into an alcohol induced coma surrounded by bushes to the sound of imaginary jack boots thumping through the undergrowth.

The sound of traffic droning close by seemed to stir some life into my aching head. My God was it aching. All that schnapps had certainly taken its toll. Eye lids flickered half open to spy the bushes that took on the appearance of a jungle. My mouth was so dry my tongue was stuck to the roof of my mouth. Where the hell was I? Self preservation kicked in as the memories of the night before started coming back. I was cold and very damp having spent the night outdoors and a very nice dew had descended on all my clothes. I felt like death warmed up as my head cleared the bushes to survey the scene. To my horror, my place of hiding was in the middle of a landscaped roundabout in the town centre. Commuters heading for work were making their way on either side of me as I ducked down to gather my thoughts. With some attempt to make myself look half human I managed to stand up, give the bush a loving pat, as if I was some horticulturalist tending their favourite shrub before heading off in the direction of the only place I knew – Onkel Paul's.

Needless to say, it was well and truly closed after a late night, so no luck there. I thought the best plan was to approach a local who was not over the age of sixteen and preferably female. They were more likely to speak English and know where the club was. After some scrutiny, I picked out my chosen Fraulein. As all English people abroad do, and I certainly did in those days, it was considered that if you spoke English very slowly, everyone would understand what you were saying, irrespective of whether they could speak English or not. Her first words (in English) were 'You look a mess, have you been sleeping rough?' She spoke better English than I did. When she realised I wasn't going to jump on her, she was very friendly and got interested when I told her I was a drummer in an English band that was going to play at the newly opened Ambassadeur Club. She thought it was hilarious when I asked if she knew where it was. Could she give me directions?

I explained the course of events from the previous night and what had happened. 'You need a coffee' was her advice and she took me to a café close by, used by all the young people from the town. The smell of German sausages was making me heave, but the coffee was good and so was the company. Her name was Heidi and she had been discussing the forthcoming opening of the club with her friends. They were excited about coming to see English bands perform when the club opened in a couple of days. It wasn't hard to see why English bands were so popular as our German counterparts had not embraced the rock n' roll culture at all. German bands still wore lederhosen with alpine hats and favoured the accordion rather than the electric guitar. Some bands had tried to capture our sound but sounded horrible and we could blow them off the stage every time.

Taken outside the Ambassadeur Club, Bad Salzuflen.

(L/R Pete, Malcolm (with Richard III hair cut), John, Bob and our friend Klaus)

The German kids loved the raw R&B sound and were even more enthusiastic when you did something crazy like jump over the drum kit to play a solo. They would shout 'Mach Show, mach show' and clap and cheer whenever we did. They were also generous enough to buy us drinks if we did a request or played to the crowd. Unlike the tight-fisted Geordies back home who wouldn't give us the steam off their pee, let alone a round of drinks. Their view was the big-headed musicians were making enough money from the club without them giving us anything else.

After a life saving coffee and a forced pastry courtesy of the lovely Heidi, we said 'Goodbye' and she promised to come to the opening night. Her directions were spot on and I managed to climb the back stairs up to our sleeping quarters for a few hours sleep. The sight that confronted me was not a pretty one to say the least. I was half glad I had found the roundabout. It was obvious that all the boys had been ill and the smell of vomit hung in the air, only just hanging below the smell of stale bodies, sweaty socks and dead farts. Poor Bob had faired worst and such was his distress, his sick had turned black. I was grateful for the coffee and fresh air which had helped me a lot. It was now around 8.30am and tried to tidy the place up a bit and open some windows to try and fumigate the room. I didn't want to end up on the street again.

After making the room look slightly less like a bomb had exploded in it and with some fresh air swirling round the room, I jumped into my bed ready for a nice sleep to get myself back on track.

Just then the owner knocked on the door and came up to see us. 'Well' he said, 'What a fine mess you have got yourselves into'. He wanted us to help him get the club ready and as he was paying us for the month, he felt it fair that we should work on the days we were not playing. It wasn't our fault they were late in opening, but he was a nice guy and it would give us something to do. It just so happened that then wasn't the right time. I managed to wake the boys and get some coffee into them and slowly they came around one by one. Malcolm appeared from under his duvet and another blonde head appeared next to his. Unbelievable, in all the mayhem he had still managed to pull a girl and get her back to the room.

Chapter Eight

The club was a converted cinema and booths had been built all around the edges with pine wood. Isaac wanted a sort of burnt wood effect on the pine, so we were given blow torches and set to work. We soon got the finishing touches to the club and it was all set to open. We had found a couple of cheap places to eat and we also had a small kitchen in the sleeping quarters, although none of us possessed much culinary skill. Once we got down to playing, it would be none stop until the end of the month anyway.

The night arrived and Isaac was very nervous about how popular the place would be. Its problem was that it was in a small place and its success would depend on whether he could attract the young people from other towns including Bielefeld which was the biggest neighbouring town. There were enough people coming through the door and by the time we took to the stage for our first set, all the booths were full and as soon as we started playing, the floor filled up and we were off. I was also pleased to see Heidi and her friends had made it and we exchanged smiles throughout the night. At the first major break, which was at 10pm when all the under 18s had to leave, I made my way over to her booth and joined them for a beer. Of course, not far behind me was Malcolm, who was like a dog on heat at the thought of new conquests. The night was a success and everyone was pleased, not least ourselves, as we were very happy to be back playing again. Heidi seemed reluctant to leave and held my hand under the table. It was obvious she didn't want to leave and I told her I would see her when we had finished. When the night was over I headed over to Heidi's table and we sat and talked. I finally drank a well-earned bottle of pilsner. Now I had more confidence, I asked her if she wanted to stay. I did point out that the accommodation was less than private but she was happy to stay. We made our way up to our rooms and settled in for the night. She was very sweet and after all that had gone before with the stress of Hamburg, she was a warm comfort to a young man. Somehow, we managed to block out the fact that the other boys were close by. I guess we were both in need of love and affection and we made love without guilt or shame.

I awoke the following morning and she had gone. I did not see her again, even though I tried to find her and asked many people who came to the club if they knew her. I discovered in that moment that intimate encounters were not merely one-night stands and emotionally I had to relate to the girl I was with. A very old-fashioned notion and much to the amusement of Malcolm, as he added another photograph to his collection.

Now that we were settled and off and running the next job was for us to buy a van of some sort. We needed transport to get us to the next engagement and we only had a limited budget. Isaac very kindly advanced us some of our money from the months work and with the help of Arnde, Malcolm and Bob they went off with Isaac in his Mercedes to see what they could get. Peter and I waited anxiously for them to return and after a few hours they came back to the club in two vehicles, one of which was our new 'van'. It was called a 'Bullie' van and was quite literally a long wheeled based mini. It was obvious that the one thing not in abundance was space. It would be a real squeeze to get us and all the gear into the van at the same time. We did a try out during the following day and the bad news for me was that my bass drum would have to be strapped to the roof rack. The thought of my beautiful Ludwig bass drum hurtling off into the night across some autobahn did not fill me with happy thoughts. I was assigned rope duty when the time came to leave.

Outside the Ambassadeur Club, Bad Salzuflen with the infamous Bullie Van. Looking at it now it is hard to believe we got all our equipment and five people in it! (L/R John, Bob and Pete)

The month passed by quite uneventfully and we were a lot more settled now we had transport of a sort and no problems with accommodation. We were visiting Onkel Paul's when we could, although we were playing every night so we would go there for an early drink and a quick bite to eat before heading into a full night through until 2am. Being in the sticks, the club didn't stay open until 6am in the morning like the Hamburg clubs did, so our work load wasn't so heavy. Close to Bad Salzuflen was the town of Herford and it contained a large English army garrison. That meant that a lot of soldiers made their way to the Ambassadeur club on a regular basis and we made friends with a lot of them. One particular character was a guy known to us as 'Joe the Drums'. He was always pissed when we saw him and one-night Peter spotted him dropping something in his pint. Peter asked him what it was and he pointed out that by putting a sugar lump in the drink it helped get you pissed quicker, especially when you didn't have a lot of money.

The club was closed on Sundays and we arranged to go to the camp at Herford and play at the NCOs' mess of the 7th Signals regiment. A mighty ten tonner arrived to take the equipment and we had a great night. Lots of English food and beer and a good crowd who danced all night to our music. We made the journey regularly on a Sunday during that month and a good time was had by us all.

Isaac announced early in the month with some pride that had had booked the No 1 German band called The Rattles for a one-night stand to put the club on the map. We were intrigued. We had seen photos of them and they were all leather trousers and big hair. When the day came for them to play, they certainly had all the right gear and most enviably, a very large Mercedes van which made ours look like a toy. There was a big crowd in that night and it was obvious a lot of people had travelled from miles around for the event. I guess from that point of view it was a success. We stormed the first part of the evening, aware that they were watching us from the side of the stage. This made us perform even better and our stage presence went through the roof that night. When it was their turn to play, the roles were reversed as we stood and watched them. We thought they were quite old fashioned and were disappointed with them. It gave us huge confidence if this was the No 1 band in Germany.

We had to finish off the night doing the morning shift until 2am that night and we stormed the stage again. I think the crowd realised that we were giving them a good run for their money and they started to cheer every song we played. We rammed all our best songs into that last set and played a blinder. They didn't want us to finish but the club had to close at 2am but we came out top dogs that night.

One-night Arnde had gone off to Onkel Paul's as he was getting bored sitting around the club every night. He had asked us to leave a key so he could get back in case we were in bed. Well, the night ended and off we went to bed completely forgetting about Arnde and the key. We all lay in bed chilling out when a stone bounced off the bedroom floor. This was followed by Arnde quietly whispering up to us 'Boys, its Arnde, please let me in'. Silence. Then suddenly a snigger came from Bob's bed and we all started to giggle as another stone hit the floor. Stone after stone found its way into the room through the window until he finally gave up, swore something terrible at us, and proceeded to fall asleep outside on an old sofa that had been left out of the back of the club. It was a foolish thing to do, as he could quite easily have taken off and we would have been stuck without a driver again. The following morning, he was not happy and I am sure the look on our faces must have told him we were lying when we said we just didn't hear him. There were enough stones on the floor to start a rock garden.

The club was doing OK, although nothing like the Funny Crow and I wondered just how long it would stay open. It was a shame, because it was a great place and the crowd were a nice friendly crowd. Thankfully their parents stayed at home with their old memories.

The weather was getting warmer and as the end of the month approached we set our sights on the next club and town we were heading for. No one knew much about Marburg and the club called the Europa Tanzdiele. We were hoping it would be a bit livelier than Bad Salzuflen. What was in store was certainly going to be 'lively' for sure, but that was to come. I eventually saw Heidi before we left and she told me she had met a local boy who she had started a relationship with and I wished her well. It was hard for me, as I had feelings for her, but how could I expect her to drop everything for me. Gone in a month and who knows where and when I would be back? I gave her a hug and she felt so good I could hardly let her go. Finally, our embrace ended and she walked off back to town. I was devastated and could not come to terms with my loss. Young love was finally tested and I bit my lip and pretended I was cool.

The final day arrived at the Ambassadeur Club and the Bully Van was loaded with our gear. I was given the job of fixing the bass drum to the roof. Thankfully it had a sturdy case but it still looked precarious despite yards of rope entwined around every slat of the roof rack. Looking inside the front of the van confirmed my suspicions that the van was really not big enough for the job and how we fitted five of us and the gear into it still remains a mystery. We bid our farewells to Isaac and his wife and wished them well with their venture. We rolled out of the car park of the Ambassadeur Club and headed south.

Arnde reckoned the journey was about 230 kilometres and would take around three hours in our illustrious van. Whatever the previous owners had used the van for, it smelt old and musty. We all smoked in those days and health and safety would have had a field day in this vehicle. No seat belts, no room and everyone lighting up on a regular basis! The windows were tiny and you could just about slide them open an inch or two for ventilation. Arnde was a big man and wide as well, so the dainty driver's seat almost disappeared when he sat on it. He was always smartly dressed and we must have been the only band in Germany who had a roadie who wore a suit with a shirt and tie. We were all very cramped and were struggling in our confined space. We had to stop several times to get out and stretch before one of us did serious damage to our bodies. With a bit of organised shuffling, we all swapped places to give parts of our bodies a rest from the cramp.

Chapter Nine

We rolled south through Paderborn, Kassel, Fritzlar, Baunatal, Borken (Hessen) and into the outskirts of Marburg. The area was very hilly and we noticed there were lots of forests around the area. Marburg seemed to stand on top of one of these hills and there appeared to be a large church on the crest of the hill. Our little blue van chugged up and down the hills, straining under the weight of Arnde, the four of us and a collection of Vox amplifiers, Farfisa organ, Ludwig drum kit and guitars. Arnde stopped and asked a few of the locals and we soon found the club, it was called the Europa Tanzdiele (European Dance Hall). It was situated at the top of a cobbled street, something Marburg seemed to have in abundance. The streets were also very narrow and winding; it reminded me of Durham City. We almost fell out of the van and I asked if it was possible to get rigor mortis whilst still alive. I was sure the first symptoms had started to kick in. The club was a good size and had a better atmosphere than the Ambassadeur. Converted cinemas were too large in my view to create an intimate atmosphere that helped the crowd enjoy live music.

We introduced ourselves to the manager of the club and loaded in the equipment. Carrying in the gear for once was quite good, as it meant we could exercise our bodies and try and get them back into normal working order. We all got cracking setting up our own gear. I was happy to remove the bass drum from the roof rack and seeing it was still in one piece! It didn't take long to get everything up and running and we had a quick sound check, as we were due to start that very night. There was no peace for the wicked and days off were a thing of the past. The club manager gave Arnde brief directions to the hotel where we were due to stay and at least with the gear unloaded, we could now get into the van without feeling like a sardine.

The hotel was just down the bottom of the cobbled street where the club was situated, so it was nice and handy at least. It looked OK and we took our cases to check in. The reception area was well appointed and had a warm homely feel. I thought I was going to enjoy this month. We duly signed in and handed over our passports for registration purposes and followed the receptionist, who had the key to our room. We were used to having one room and it was common practise to give us so-called 'family rooms' which had five beds in them. We spent most of our days and nights elsewhere, so if it was clean and the beds comfortable, we were happy. We walked on through several corridors, each one getting a little less decorated and a little less well lit. We continued through another set of doors, down a set of stairs and on through what looked like staff quarters. Across a courtyard and the room key was inserted into the door and we were in. It was a large room with bunk beds and one single bed, one small wash basin, cracked mirror, one chair and a little stove which could heat two pans. There was threadbare carpet on the floor and wall paper flaking from the walls. 'Champion bonny lad, welcome to Marburg'.

John enjoying the sumptuous en-suite and cooking facilities
at the group hotel in Marburg.

We exchanged glances and turned to confront the receptionist. She had
disappeared as fast as her German trotters could take her back into the
warmth of civilisation. Malcolm summed up the place for us all. 'This is a
fucking shit hole, I'm not staying here'. We knew that negotiation with
German club owners was futile and their lack of charity towards English
groups was legendary. Malcolm calmed down after a while and we sorted out
who was sleeping where. Arnde got the single bed as there was no way he
could manage a top bunk and may well bring down the whole thing if he
jumped into the bottom one. Someone got a pan of water boiling and we
made ourselves a cup of tea each from supplies we had brought from Bad
Salzuflen. It was a small attempt to try and make the place seem homelier. It
failed miserably!

We were missing good old British milk and as the Germans were
predominantly coffee drinkers, fresh milk was not generally available. All
they seemed to have was condensed milk which despatched a good cup of tea
to hell and back. We decided to leave the van at the hotel and walk up the
road to the club and check out the area before going to the club for our first
set. We soon discovered a good little place almost next to the club which did a

nice beer and fried egg and chips for not many Deutschmarks. After buying the van, money was a commodity we didn't have much of. We were still in catch up mode in that area and cursed Geoff daily. I think we would have throttled him if he had come anywhere near us during that time.

To add to our woes, before we had left for Germany, Geoff had arranged for us to buy a Vox 'Beatle' amplifier which served as our P.A. System. It was calculated that we could easily afford the hire purchase payments from our German earnings. Of course, that didn't consider us paying three times as much for hotels in Hamburg, an air fare to send Marie back to England and buying a bloody van as well. Bob's mother had kindly signed the agreement with Saville's Music Store in Sunderland and they were on to her now asking where the first two payments were? Needless to say, we had not had enough money to send the payments and a letter had arrived for Bob and quite understandably she was not impressed. There was a clear message that if the money was not forthcoming, then the amplifier would have to be returned or the HP Company would be paying her a visit to take possession of goods to the value of the amplifier. You can imagine that went down well with Bob's parents like a Zeppelin at an air show. We would have to somehow save enough money to get these payments off to England before Bob's mum got repossessed. It was getting harder and harder to recover from our initial set back.

We got into the club around 7pm to check out the locals before taking to the stage for our first set. It was getting full and it was obvious the club did good business. We discovered Marburg was a University town, so it was full of students from all over Germany. What was very heartening for us was that most of them seemed to be of the female variety. We loved the German girls. They seemed to be so much more mature than the English girls back home and certainly worldlier wise when it came to boys. They had a fascination with English musicians and we were soon to discover that some girls 'specialised' in either singers, bass players, drummers, guitarists and keyboard players, each taking it upon themselves to bed the respective player in each band.

This, of course, went down extremely well with us and as hot-blooded teenagers away from home, a recipe for mayhem. Malcolm was already drooling at the thought of future conquests. In such a hot bed of female talent his mission was taking on new proportions. Our first set went down well and a good sign for us was that the dance floor remained full throughout. If they didn't like you, then it would remain horribly empty and you would soon be on the road back to England. At the break, we went and got some beers and settled down for a quick ten minutes and already we were joined by some of the girls who were also buying us beers. They were fun and good looking too and we were into overdrive. By the end of the second set, we were already pairing off and things were looking good for later that night. We finished off the night at 2am and the manager said he was very pleased with us and had had good comments about us. Just keep your noses clean and keep playing like that and you'll have a good month. We asked if there was any chance of a better room at the hotel, but as we suspected, his reply was strangely a familiar one we would get accustomed to. 'All the other groups stayed there and they didn't complain'.

Chapter Ten

We left the Europe Tanzdiele club and wandered off back to the hotel with our new friends, laughing and giggling with the impending night of debauchery. Because our room was so isolated from the main hotel, it was easy for us to go around the back of the hotel and avoid the prying eyes of reception. It was certainly not going to be a night of quiet intimacy, but that didn't seem to bother the girls so we were fine. Poor Arnde, who didn't have the same pulling power as us, was stuck in the middle of the room surrounded by four English musicians getting their rocks off. It must have been very frustrating for him and sleep must not have come easy to him. The girls that Malcolm and I had got off with were obviously friends and were laughing and talking to each other in German. The night progressed and the groaning and creaking eventually subsided. Quiet fell on the room with the smell of sex lingering heavily in the air, at least as quiet as a room can be with nine people trying to sleep.

Morning came and everyone roused themselves, slowly getting their clothes together and boiling a pan for a cup of coffee. We had given up on tea. The girls had to go to work and said they would see us that night. Everyone was upbeat and looking forward to a month of partying. Later that day we went off to get some food and Malcolm and I met the two girls who had been with us. Malcolm was a little off hand with his girl, as he was ready to sample some more of what Marburg had to offer. This girl, however, had other thoughts and got quite upset when he said he didn't want to see her that night. Her friend who I was with looked at me with enquiring eyes and I said I would be happy to see her later if she was up for it. Malcolm's friend went off crying and we went back to the hotel to get ready for the night ahead.

When we arrived at the club, my girl was waiting at the entrance to the club looking upset and worried. When she saw us coming, she ran up and told me that her friend had been so upset with Malcolm she had taken a drug overdose and was now in hospital. At first, although we were concerned, we were not too worried as if she was in hospital then at least she would be OK and would get over it. Then the bombshell arrived. She told us that her friend was also the girl friend of the main Romany Gypsy leader in the area and he had gone to the hospital to find out what had happened. She had taken the overdose because she realised how angry he would be if he had found out she had slept with Malcolm. The gypsy leader now knew everything and the cause of his displeasure would be appearing live at the Europe Tanzdiele on a nightly basis.

Our hearts sunk and I must confess I felt sick with fear. We had never been involved in much trouble before. Sure, there were fights at some of the dances we played at when rival boys from neighbouring mining villages would visit the next village looking for trouble, but this was on another level. You just knew you didn't cross Romany Gypsies because they would seek a horrible revenge. It was hard to imagine how we had got into such a situation so easily. Of all the girls in the town, Malcolm had to pick that one. To be fair, they had picked us and they had done all the chasing.

The other problem we had, was that all our gear was in the club and if we went in and packed up and left before the end of our agreement, the club would sue us and we would certainly never get another work permit to work in Germany again. We had a meeting and decided we just had to continue. Surely the guy would have other things to do and it would blow over.

On stage at the Europa Tanzdiele Club, Marburg, Germany 1966

Not a chance. That brought us to the second set and we were playing Spencer Davis's - 'Somebody Help Me'. The night had gone well until the gypsy gang turned up at the club and surrounded the stage. As soon as we left the stage after the end of our set, the 50-strong gang made their way to the side of the stage to confront us. Arnde, our dear roadie, was as white as a sheet and was the only one who could speak with them, as none of them spoke English. They were all olive skinned, wearing droopy black moustaches, open necked shirts, leather waist coats and jeans. Their long oily black hair made them look like pirates. Their dark eyes seemed to be filled with hatred and that hatred was most certainly directed towards us. The leader was clearly older than the rest and looked like the girl's father rather than her boy friend. Arnde was sweating as the discussion got heated, none of us aware of what was being said and whether we were going to get out of this alive.

Taken during a break at the Europa Tanzdiele in Marburg 1966. Shortly after this photograph was taken England beat Germany in the World Cup and we had to hide the Union Jack stickers!

The club owner refused to call the police on the basis that he didn't want his club wrecked and he had to live with this lot when we were gone. We weren't sure just what he meant by 'gone' but at the time, it had a very permanent sound to it. To buy some time, with a stroke of genius, Arnde offered to buy them all a beer. Unbelievably that seemed to break the tension a little. The men closest to their leader were obviously his henchmen and kept showing us their knives and guns tucked into their trousers. So apart from being about to be murdered, we were now being rendered bankrupt having to buy 50 bloody beers at club prices. The things that were now flying through our minds – death, bankruptcy, Bob's mum having her home repossessed, our parents having to come to Marburg and collect our bodies; could it get any worse?

There was a delay while all the bottles of beer were served and the atmosphere got slightly more relaxed. We were beside ourselves, as we couldn't get out of Arnde what the hell was going on. He looked like death and just kept talking to the leader. We were due to go back on but the club owner kept behind his bar, no doubt counting out how much he had made from us in one bar order. The crowd had thinned, as they had obviously sussed something was going on and to be fair, who would want to socialise with 50 avenging gypsies apart from us?

Suddenly, there seemed to be an impasse and the leader stood up, said something to Arnde, turned on his heels and left. His entourage followed closely behind him leaving a large amount of beer bottles, all sadly empty. Arnde wiped his forehead to remove the cold sweat that had gathered like a sea of terror on is brow. 'Fucking hell boys, why did I ever agree to work for you?' 'Can you imagine what I have just been through in the last 15 minutes'?

He wouldn't discuss what had been said, but told us that the leader had left to think about what he should do with us. We had to resume our playing to see out the night and our eyes did not leave the entrance to the club for very long. Every time the door opened our hearts stopped, expecting retribution to walk through at any moment.

At the end of the night we held a summit meeting and we decided we should pack up and leave. Whatever trouble we would be in with the club did not compare to being shot. We discussed this with the owner and he understood and said he did not blame us, as these were very bad people. It was always good to get a reassuring word from a friend. We left the club to return to the hotel and agreed we would go back in the morning for the gear. What the hell had we got ourselves into? Hamburg was bad enough, but this was serious shit.

When we got back to the hotel, we all tried to sleep without much success. We chatted, trying to keep our spirits up and we were all in bed fully clothed. Such was our fear that we even felt vulnerable undressed. Dawn broke and as soon as we could, packed our cases and drove to the club. We had a coffee in the café next to the club waiting for the owner to arrive. We didn't know what we were going to do or where we would go. We only knew we had to leave Marburg to survive. Our next gig was two weeks away and we would not be earning any money to pay for a hotel. Suddenly the roundabout in Bad Salzuflen seemed like a sanctuary.

Shortly after ten in the morning, the club owner arrived and he even looked happy. He had a smile on his face. 'You are not going to believe this' he said, 'but your gypsy friend got into a big fight when he left the club last night and is seriously hurt in hospital'. The owner said he would be in hospital for several weeks so you need not worry, he won't bother you now. Also, several of his gang have been hurt, so they have other things to worry about. Apparently when they left the club, they had gone to a bar where they drank regularly and had been confronted by a rival gypsy gang and there had been a big fight between them. Several stabbings and one-person shot had been the outcome of the fight and the police had also made several arrests. We weren't convinced and did remind the owner that he had refused to call the police when it looked like we were about to get done.

He assured us that everything would be alright and we reluctantly agreed to stay. However, we wanted regular updates as to the progress in hospital of our friend in case he made a rapid recovery and wanted revenge, somehow blaming us for his misfortune. We returned to the hotel, still uneasy, and reminded Malcolm to keep his pistol in his pocket until we returned to Hamburg. That morning Bob and I decided to go for a long walk to get some air and take in the situation. We walked for a long time and what seemed to be mostly uphill. After a couple of hours, we came upon the large church that we had seen when we had first approached Marburg at the beginning of the month. This was St Elizabeth's Church and it was a beautiful old building and we were drawn inside. The atmosphere was so calm and restful and we felt for the first time in days to be safe. We both, without saying anything to each other, took a seat in one of the pews and sat in silence, both in silent prayer. I have never felt as close to God as in this moment. I honestly thanked him for getting us out of the mess we had got ourselves into and to give us strength to face the challenges ahead. I could have stayed there forever. Only the day before, I had felt utterly lost and alone, totally terrified and in genuine fear for my life. I felt we had been spared for some reason, and that reason was known only by Him.

It was only an act of fate that had saved us. We were not completely out of the woods yet, but so far so good. The manager of the club was getting daily reports from a contact he had in the hospital and our friend was making slow progress. He had, by all accounts, been given a severe beating with several ribs broken. That could well have been our fete. Eventually we dragged ourselves out of the church and reluctantly headed back to the town and reality. It was like walking back into a horror movie.

We still felt very uneasy and the end of the month couldn't arrive quickly enough. We decided to keep as low a profile as possible for the remainder of the month and apart from when we were on stage, would keep out of sight. We noticed at the local cinema a Clint Eastwood film was doing the rounds and had heard from home that everyone was going mad about his new film called 'A Fistful of Dollars'. This had only made it to Germany and we decided to go and see it. It was good to disappear into the darkness of the cinema for a few hours and be unseen. It was strange to see Clint Eastwood ride into town, throw back his poncho and suddenly say 'Das ist gut mein Herr' to the Mexican bandits mocking him from outside the saloon. We really enjoyed the escapism of the moment, although seeing people getting shot didn't exactly settle the nerves either.

We were quite cut off from home and English news in general. There had, however, been quite a lot of talk about the Football World Cup which had been going on for some weeks. Football wasn't that interesting to us then, but the final was being held at Wembley and England had made the final against, oh my God – Germany. Great, here we were in the middle of enemy territory and now we must play them at bloody football. We could tell there was a real excitement building and in 1966, as we had discovered, the Second World War still had deep memories for a lot of Germans. Now was their chance to avenge for the defeat in 1945, they could at last humble the British and put them in their place.

The final was due to be played at Wembley on Saturday 30th July 1966 and we had found a place close to the hotel where they had a television set that worked and were making a big deal of showing the game. It was absolutely rammed with Germans and was a long bar which held around 500 people. The bar was at the back of the hall serving masses of pilsner, the waitresses carrying jug after jug to the thirsty horde. We decided to slip in once the match had started and stay at the back near the door. We got ourselves a beer and thankfully everyone was facing forward, stretching to see the television relaying the action in glorious black and white.

No one noticed our arrival so we were happy. Germany dominated the opening of the game and then on twelve minutes Helmet Haller scored for Germany through an error by Ray Wilson. The crowd went mad and bottles of beer were being thrown everywhere. Four Englishmen remained silent at the bar. Perhaps we should have cheered a little bit to try and disguise our identity, as six minutes later Geoff Hurst header in the equaliser. 'Come one, game on' Malcolm sang as he punched the air. Four reasonably lively Englishmen expressed a small delight while 500 German football supporters remained stone cold silent. This wasn't quite going as well as we had expected.

The half time whistle went and we slipped out of the door into the street for a breather. We realised that we needed to keep quiet if England scored again as we were severely outnumbered. We waited for the second half to get under way and slipped back inside the smoky room. England were playing much better in the second half and in the seventy eighth minute Hurst had a shot blocked but Martin Peters came steaming in and put the loose ball into the net. This time we all took a deep drink of lager and said nothing. The crowd were not happy now and there were a lot of sideways glances in our direction. The clock was now ticking down to full time and the atmosphere was tense. I was suggesting we leave before the final whistle and then suddenly the Swiss referee, Dienst, awarded Germany a free kick just outside the box. I can't watch. The free kick was taken and there is a mix up in the box and Weber scores - 2-2. Full time and the Germans go mad. We now must play extra time and another tidal wave of pilsner makes its way down the length of the bar. We have shrunk in size now and trying to be invisible.

Extra time gets under way and the nerves are jangling, not to mention the pots of pilsner. England go on the attack and on ninety-eight minutes, Alan Ball sends in a cross and Hurst shoots. The ball cannons into the bottom of the crossbar and drops down just behind the line. Well, according to Russian linesman Bakhramov, it was behind the line and goal is given. The Germans go bloody mental and it looks like the television set is about to be smashed to pieces. There are scuffles at the front of the bar as some of the locals want to see the end of the match, not a television being smashed to pieces. I am looking at the door and working my way slowly towards it as I have no intention of staying here for much longer. The German football team are giving their all and play is now end to end stuff until just before the end of extra time Geoff Hurst seals the victory with a blinding strike and gives him a world cup hat trick.

We are almost at the door to slip out when Malcolm drops his glass and it smashes in a million pieces all over the floor. That seems to be the trigger for the entire crowd's anger as they rise to their feet and start heading in our direction. We are out of there in seconds and running as fast as we can up the road pursued by a very angry mob of German football supporters. The local streets being narrow and bendy assist our escape and as our hotel accommodation is situated in the depths of its buildings, we can give the crowd the slip ducking into a small alley and through a gap in a fence to relative safety.

We crash onto our bunks, red faced and panting. I haven't run that fast in my entire life. Can this month hold any more twists and turns for us? Tomorrow is our last day in this place and right now I am going to pack. We decide that as soon as we play the last set tomorrow night, we will pack the gear and drive through the night to Hamburg. We are back at the Funny Crow and we can't wait to return.

We turn up at the club that night and realise our kit is sporting quite a few Union Jack stickers which we picked up from the British Army. We decide it will be better to cover them up and not antagonise the locals who may well still be licking their heels from their World Cup defeat. Luckily the night goes without incident and we are now getting excited about the prospect of leaving Marburg.

There was a good crowd that night and many of the locals seem sorry to see us go. At 2am we wearily start packing up all the gear and humping it all outside to start the complicated process of getting it all in the van. Our suitcases have got smaller since leaving Sunderland due to the lack of space in the van. The club owner thanks us for the month and we all nervously laugh at our close escape. He thought he was going to have his club wrecked as well, so we all consider ourselves lucky. He pays us the balance of our money which is considerably diminished due to the purchase of 50 or so beers. German club owners were not known for their kindness and the full charge is made on the statement.

Once again, my bass drum sits on top of the roof rack and as I tighten the rope holding it on, I wonder if I will ever see it again. It's now 3.30am and we're all shattered. We all squeeze into the van and Arnde starts it up ready to leave. As the van slowly gains pace down the cobbled road we feel elated that we are eventually leaving Marburg and in one piece. This place will haunt us forever. We all vow never ever to return whatever the circumstances. We have 400 kilometres to go and in this van, it will take around six hours. Arnde heads for Hannover and to the autobahn north towards Hamburg. We ask Arnde if he knows anyone in Hamburg with a large tin opener. By the time we get to Hamburg we figure it will be the only way of getting out of the van. As we drift off into a restless sleep, Bob farts; which sets the tone for the rest of the journey.

Chapter Eleven

Thankfully the weather is warm being August, which is just as well as the van doesn't have a heater. We have had to stop just outside of Hannover to change positions and get something to eat. It is 6am and we all feel like shit. I can't help thinking that Cliff Richard would not be doing this, and somehow, we have to improve our lot or we are all going to jack this in. After a coffee, bratwurst and cigarette, we get back on the road and hope we can get to Hamburg in good time. The van is not happy having to carry so much weight and Arnde is not at all confident with its reliability. He certainly saw himself sitting behind the wheel of a gleaming new Ford Transit rather than this post war mechanical heap.

With a fair wind we reach Hamburg without any breakdowns although we have had to fill the radiator with water several times. The sight of Hamburg and the suburb of Grindelberg fills our hearts with joy. It is like coming home and we know we will be even more popular with the Funny Crow crowd. We have heard there was a big cheer when it was announced we were coming back.

As Arnde lives in Hamburg, he has been able to arrange for us to stay at a nice small hotel very near to the club. The other good news is that he has been able to negotiate a much better rate as we are staying for a month. We get to Hamburg at midday and go straight to the hotel to get rid of the cases. The hotel is nice and we have a large room in the basement with four single beds. That will do, although we find the bathroom is on the second floor so a bit of a hike for that. Thankfully there is a washbasin with hot and cold water in our room so compared with Marburg, this is luxury.

After claiming our beds, we freshen up and go straight to the club to unload the gear and get set up. Bob is greeted by a letter from his Mum which has been sent to the Funny Crow as she didn't have our address in Marburg. She has had to pay the payments on the Vox amplifier system and is not very happy. We all agree we need to get some money over to her as soon as we get our first week's money. Alexander greets us like long lost friends and says the crowd are looking forward to having us back. This cheers us up a lot and we set about getting all the gear into the club.

We have a sound check and everyone is playing like they are up for this. We also decide we will get some new songs learnt, as we can get into the club during the day. Arnde has a new portable record player and a few new tunes in the repertoire will liven up the sets. We go back to the hotel and crash out for a couple of hours. It has been a long night and an even longer day. We have six hours of playing ahead of us so some rest is needed. We give Arnde some money and he goes off to get us some chicken and chips which is a popular dish of the day.

We get back to the club around six thirty and to our surprise there is a large queue of people snaking their way around the corner and disappearing off into Grindelallee. It seems that our reputation has grown and this is something that at first, we find hard to believe. From the moment we launched into our first number, the club was heaving and the crowd were cheering and laughing, obviously having a really good time. It was brilliant to be so popular and Alexander was beaming from ear to ear as business was obviously going to be very good for him this month.

The first night goes an absolute storm and sets the tone for the rest of the month. Trays of drinks keep flowing to the stage, scotch and cokes are the popular drink of the day, but we maintain a discipline not to get drunk. We didn't want to spoil a good thing and after the last month's trauma, we're all agreed heads down and for once have some fun. After all, that was what got us here in the first place. We decide to head back to the hotel after the last set as we are exhausted. It is the height of summer in Hamburg and with the sun shining on a regular basis during the day it gives us an incentive to get up earlier than usual and explore. Having Arnde as a road manager helped, especially as he is a 'Hamburger'. We finally get to see the Reeperbahn with all the sex clubs and the famous Herbertstrasse, also known as the 'Street of Windows'. The prostitutes could be quite hostile if they sussed you were just there to look and not pay for sex. It was quite an education for us and we were all growing up very fast.

We take a stroll to the Top Ten Club, which is situated at 136 Reeperbahn, and even though it was during the day, we ventured in and managed to have a quick peep inside. It looked great and had a sunken dance floor in the middle of the club. The other thing we noticed was it had its own PA system, with big speakers above and at the side of the stage together with studio quality Sennheiser microphones. We all hoped that one day we would get a booking there and with our increasing popularity at the Funny Crow, the bush drums were beating about us around the Hamburg circuit. At the end of the Reeperbahn is the biggest music store we have ever seen. It was called Music City and it was like an Aladdin's Cave to us. It was a pity we were broke and couldn't buy anything. It was still good to look around the store and try out some of the new gear.

That night we were in the middle of our first set when I started to smell burning to my left. Sat next to me at the back of the stage was the 'Beatle' Vox amplifier that we were using as a PA system. Suddenly there is a bang and the amplifier blew up, and the PA went dead. We take a short break to sort out the problem, which given the bang, we know is not going to be solved easily. A horrible molten liquid had leaked from the bottom of the amp down onto the big speaker cabinet, smearing all over the familiar Vox speaker cloth. For the short term, we must route the mikes through the other amplifiers which was not ideal.

The following day Arnde takes the amplifier to a friend of his who repairs electrical goods and luckily, he can mend it. The cost is not cheap, but we are relieved all round that we don't have to buy a new one. This is especially pleasing as we haven't even paid for this one yet! The fact is Bob's Mum has more right to use the amplifier than we do. We get back to the club in the afternoon and set up the Vox amp and have a good rehearsal adding four new numbers to the set. We have all had the 'Hamburg' throat again given the longs hours we are playing but we soon recover. Back in the UK, we would normally be tucked up in bed by midnight. In Germany, the clubs would be open until 6am, especially those in Hamburg. The upside was that the band's vocals had become strong with the amount of time we actually sang and the voice box got tougher and more resilient. We also all smoked then; it was the thing to do in the sixties and were never made aware of the harmful effects it could have on your health.

We had discovered a local Chinese restaurant just around the corner to the club called the Dsching Gao. We were getting sick of German food and there is only so many bratwurst and sauerkraut you could eat, as nice as it may be. With our limited budget, we could only afford special fried rice each and a coke. The manager and waiters must have thought we were weird ordering such a limited amount and the same dish every time we went there. The food tasted so good and the mound of rice, peas, chicken, pork and prawns was a feast for us. We were really starting to miss things like soft white English bread, proper bacon and a Sunday roast.

The conversation round the table started to get on to the subject of us all being homesick. Also, we had not yet been offered another month's work, although we felt our German agent would come up with something. The other problem for us was the van, which was clearly a short-term option given the lack of space it offered when fully loaded with us and the gear. We made the decision to return to England at the end of the month so we could get ourselves sorted and make sure our affairs were put back in order. Having made the decision, it seemed to take a weight off our shoulders somehow. We would discuss the finer details later and having paid for our meal; we left the restaurant feeling well fed and happy to be returning home in three weeks time.

Later that week, we were playing a set around midnight, when we noticed a new arrival at the bar in the Funny Crow. Somehow, he just looked English, but he seemed to be taking an interest in us from his bar stool. You can tell a lot of things from the stage looking out on to an audience, reading peoples faces and their reactions. It becomes an instinct. At the end of the set he wandered over to the stage and introduced himself. 'Hi guys, I'm Ricky Barnes and I book the bands at the Top Ten Club'. We nearly fainted! This was one of the top music men in Hamburg and he had come to check us out. He was a Scottish saxophone player, as we later learned, and he regularly got on stage with the bands and joined in with them for a couple of numbers. He was a real character. We went to the bar for a drink with him and we got on well. He said he liked the band and would we be interested in a month's residency?

We were really flattered, but had to explain that we were going back to the UK at the end of the month. He said not to worry and as soon as we got back to Hamburg he would be happy to fit us in somewhere. This gave us a great boost and as he bid his farewells, we finished that night on a real high. We were also getting on famously with the girls in Hamburg who seemed a lot less complicated than those in Marburg. The rooms we had at the hotel where we were staying in were in the basement of the building. It was very handy for the hotel to keep four English musicians conveniently out of the way whilst still taking their money. It was also handy for us, because we could get our visitors into the rooms without them having to go through the reception area and the watchful eye of the manager.

Another visitor to the club was a lady called Helga Boddin. She was a producer for NDR, the main radio service for North Germany and had heard from her friends about our popularity at the Funny Crow. She produced a radio show called 'Twen Club Im Studio 1' that had live bands on it. She asked us if we would like to do a show for her. We were delighted and she booked us there and then for the following week's show. It was going to help our status in Germany by doing such a prestigious show and Alex agreed to let us start later that night, as we would not get back from the recording until around 8pm.

We duly arrived at the large building that was the headquarters of NDR in Rothenbaumchaussee. It was just around the corner from the Funny Crow in Grindelberg so it would not take us long to get back after the show. The radio studios were very modern with all the best equipment. The show was done from their biggest studio because it had to accommodate the live audience. After setting up, the engineer miked us all up and I had microphone all over the kit. We did one number for levels until the engineer was satisfied. A short while later the audience arrived and most of them were all from the Funny Crow. Eventually the show started and on the red light, the announcer welcomed everyone to the 'Twen Club' and introduced us and we were on air live. It was frightening but also exhilarating at the same time, knowing that we were playing live to most of Northern Germany.

The show went very well and it was a good experience for us all. Peter's girlfriend at the time got her father to record the show which we could listen to later that week.

We had to start making plans for our journey home. It was obvious that all of us could not make such a monumental journey in the van without someone getting seriously disfigured. It was decided that two of us would have to go home via train and ferry. This was the best option for the lucky two, so we put our names in a hat and Arnde was given the task of drawing out two papers. The job was done and I lit up and took a long drag from my Ernte 23 cigarette. The tension was high and his large stubby hand dipped into the hat and out came the first piece of paper. Arnde looked pleased as he read 'Bob'. Bob looked even happier as he slumped back on the bed, his journey settled. We all looked nervously towards Arnde as in went the hand again. He unrolled the paper slowly and paused, then looked at Malcolm and said 'John'. Malcolm and Pete groaned, but it was obviously fair, as Arnde would not have considered fixing the outcome, he was too straight for that. I was very pleased to be making the journey with Bob, I think if Arnde had pulled out Malcolm, I would have volunteered for the van.

Bob and I still felt guilty, because we knew the journey would be a difficult one for the other, but we did win fair and square. Arnde sorted out the railway tickets. We would get a train directly from Hamburg, which would take us to the Hook of Holland. The ferry would take us to Harwich and then a train from Harwich to London and across London by tube to Kings Cross. The last leg of the journey would be a train to Durham where we would then be picked up and taken to Sunderland. We had a week left before we were due back and mentally we were all half way home already. The week ended well and again Alex was very pleased with the business we had done for him over the month. He makes us promise to come back, as he will book us straight away.

We have a bit of a party on the last night back at the hotel and make the most of our Hamburg girls. We remembered how restrained the English girls were back home compared to the lovely fräuleins. Morning arrives and the hotel room is a mess. Four months of limited laundry had taken its toll. Peter decided against taking back his underwear, which had turned a curious green colour. I think he was worried that it might manifest itself into some great monster in the back of the van and devour them on their journey back home. We all pitied the poor refuse collector who would be unfortunate to come across Peter's little parcel. Our suitcases were packed as best we could and loaded into the van. Somehow, the space which would have been occupied by Bob and I didn't seem to make a lot of difference.

We said good bye to the girls who cried as we left. Even though we were homesick, we also felt sad to be leaving too. The little blue van made its weary way through central Hamburg to drop us off at the large railway station for our train which was due to leave at 10.30 in the morning. Arnde took us inside to make sure we got the correct train. The station was huge and very imposing with a very high ceiling. For us, it was a place as dark and foreboding as you could imagine. I felt like I was on the run from Colditz Castle and any minute some German guard would ask me for my papers which would be forged, of course. The ticket collector at the gate was dressed like a five-star General. We had noticed, in the time we had been in Germany, they still loved a uniform. Even postmen looked like Generals. I guess old habits die hard.

We said goodbye to Arnde, Malcolm and Pete and found our seats in the right compartment. We would not move too far from these seats until we arrived in the Hook of Holland. The boys walked off back to the van, looking back once with a look of envy, as they started their arduous trip back to the UK. They would have to drive from Hamburg back to Calais and then across the Channel to Dover. The last leg of the journey was a 350-mile drive from Dover to Sunderland. A massive drive in the old van we had. Not the shortest route of course, but the cheapest. It would take them nearly eight hours to drive from Dover to Sunderland.

Chapter Twelve

The whistle blew and our train slowly moved out of the station. Before long we were rolling through the outskirts of Hamburg towards Bremen and then on to Osnabruck into the Netherlands. We drifted in and out of sleep and chatted about everything to keep from getting too bored. The conversation drifted to how we had started at the Youth Club in Sunderland and how it was hard to believe where we had come since then. We also kept thinking of the boys in the van making their way slowly back to the UK and hoped they would be alright.

As the train chugged on, we realised we were close to Holland as the land started to level out into a flat landscape. We even started to see the windmills scatted around the countryside. The train terminal at the Hook of Holland was right in the docks and it was a short walk to the ferry terminal. We were hungry and tired and the wind whipping off the sea was cold and unwelcoming. The skies were darkening and rain was in the air. It did not look great for a channel crossing. The ferries that were docked seemed to lift with the swell and the ropes holding them to the quay groaned with the strain.

Our tickets and passports were checked and we embarked up the gangway which was swaying violently in the wind. We made for the cafeteria on board and treated ourselves to a coffee and a cheese sandwich. The first refreshment we had taken since leaving Hamburg. Soon the ropes were being thrown to the ground of the docks as the ferry broke away and headed for the English Channel. As soon as we broke from the harbour, it was obvious we were in for a very bumpy ride. The ferry was rolling over the waves like a roller coaster and everything loose was being thrown from one side of the ship to the other. We were hanging on to the table which was thankfully screwed to the floor. Movement anywhere was almost impossible, and a visit to the toilets was a major exercise in acrobatics. People were throwing up everywhere and turning the ship into a scene from Armageddon. We weren't sure if several months of exposure to German food had anything to do with it, but we were fine in that area and tucked into another cheese sandwich. People close by were not impressed and turned even greener.

After what seemed like a lifetime, the English coast and the White Cliffs were finally in view. The closer we got, the quieter the sea became. It was good to see the old place again and as we docked, even the seagulls seemed to be squawking in English. Once the gangway was lowered, we led the way followed by very green looking travellers. We noted with some amusement that one of our fellow travellers, who sported a very full beard, still had a piece of carrot embedded in the foliage. We laughed all the way through customs!

We were now on English soil and back on an English train. It was easy to tell, because the train was dirty and it left Harwich late. We fell asleep almost immediately the train left Harwich and didn't wake up until we were close to arriving at Liverpool Street Station. We took the underground to King's Cross and checked trains to Durham. Thankfully there was a train waiting on a platform, so we could go and get some seats. I got some English coins out of the bottom of my suitcase and rang home to tell them what time we would be in Durham. It was great to hear Mum's voice and she had my uncle on standby to come and collect us.

We were finally on the homeward stretch and as the train left King's Cross, we at last felt we were on home turf and not so far from home now. All the stations we passed through had familiar names and when we arrived in York it was the last big step before Durham. The approach to Durham is quite spectacular as the train loops round the big viaduct bringing into sight the castle, the cathedral and the River Wear. As the train came to a halt, the brakes screeched and it finally came to a halt. I could see Mum and my uncle waiting for us and we were off the train. After hugs and a quick 'Have you been eating properly', we were in the car and off down the A1 towards Sunderland and home. We dropped Bob off at his house in Pallion and I arranged to see him the following day to hopefully welcome home the others. We had arranged for them to go straight to Bob's house as Arnde would be staying with them.

Boy it was good to be home. I tucked in to some real fish and chips, white bread and a proper cup of tea. It was possibly the best meal I ever ate. We sat and talked for ages about what we had been up to, well with some careful editing. It would not have done to be too honest, or I would not have been allowed to go back. Finally, it was off upstairs to my own bed, the crisp white sheets and blankets. It all felt very odd as we had become used to the continental quilts or duvets that were commonplace in Germany. The UK was yet to discover this marvellous invention. I managed to find a gap in the sheets and pulled myself in. Within seconds I had drifted into a deep sleep.

I awoke with a startle as at first, I did not know where I was. It was with some relief that I was in my own room and the smell of grilled bacon was enough to get my bones out of bed and down the stairs. After the fish and chips, the joy of a bacon butty and mug of tea with fresh milk was a perfect and proper start to the day. It was also good watching English television and reading the paper again. After a delightful hot bath, I noted that my clothes were already in the washing machine. Mum had set the machine to 'kill' judging by the temperature it had been set to. She obviously decided that anything less than boil would not do the job of removing several months of German grime.

Bob lived in Pallion, which was about a ten-minute walk from my home. I set off the meet him and wait for Pete, Malcolm and Arnde to hopefully arrive.

When I got to his house, he told me he had had a call from them at Dover and they expected to be in Sunderland early evening – van permitting. They also mentioned that the exhaust had blown when they were driving through Belgium and were all basket cases with the noise. They also had trouble persuading the ferry operator at Calais to allow the van on board. They had a rule that all cars and vehicles had to be roadworthy before they could embark. Our little 'Bully' van failed on several counts, not just the exhaust.

As the sun started to go down behind the row of terraced houses, the smoke from the coal fires made its way skywards out of the house chimneys, the sound came. Quiet at first and the sound was distinctly alien to us. As the minutes ticked by it got louder and louder and sounded like an invasion. We went outside into Tamerton Street and in the distance, we could hear the most outrageous racket. By the time the little blue van spluttered around the corner you couldn't hear yourself think. The look of abject horror on the occupant's faces said it all. How they had endured that noise for so long, I will never know. We helped them out of their cocoon and soon they were in Bob's front room supping on mugs of tea. I have never seen three people looked so shattered in all my life. Peter was still bent double, as he had sat in the back for most of the journey.

Their journey had been worse than anticipated and the van had not performed well. I guess it was a journey too far and having to transport three people and all that gear had been too much. I must confess I was relieved to see my bass drum still firmly strapped to the roof rack. The boys were now anxious to get home and we dispersed for the rest of the day. We had arranged to rehearse the following day at Bob's to get back into the routine. We had already contacted our agent who had filled our diary with lots of clubs and dances. Of course, we were now being billed as 'Direct from Hamburg's Top Ten Club' which the promoters felt added some extra credibility to our name.

Our main priority was to get a replacement van, as it was universally considered the 'Bully' van was as good as dead. I don't think we could have persuaded any of us to get back into it, even at gun point! We used the first gig money we got to put a deposit on a second-hand Austin J4 van with Bob's mum signing the hire purchase agreement again! How we managed to persuade her to do that, after the Vox amplifier situation, remains a mystery. I guess we owed our respective parents a great deal, as they had stood by us throughout.

The J4 at least had plenty of room and could accommodate all the gear and us which made a nice change. As we discovered, it would take Arnde some time to get used to driving an English vehicle on the 'wrong' side of the road. Driving through to South Shields one night for a gig at a working men's club, we approached a roundabout at the end of a long dual carriageway and he proceeded to turn right and go around it the wrong way! This was compounded by the fact it was landscaped and we couldn't see if anything was coming. Much abuse and screaming occurred as we sailed round expecting to have a head on collision at any moment. Thankfully nothing came and we escaped, but it certainly focused Arnde's mind and ours. Was I ever going to see my eighteenth birthday?

Over the coming weeks, we managed to get some new songs rehearsed, so our sets were up to date. The charts were scanned and we would be off down to Saville's in Holmeside in the town centre to buy the chart records. By now, it was 45 rpm singles and not a 78rpm in sight. Bob's front room or mine was used by us to rehearse. It was amazing, but no one ever complained. We had quite an impressive repertoire now, having had to play so long in Germany. It was also very strange for us now finishing at 10.30pm having only played two forty-five minute sets. In Germany we would be just getting started playing through until 5/6am in the morning. It was very different for us adapting back into the UK club's way. We had plenty of dates booked in and apart from doing all the North-East clubs, we would also play at youth clubs, the Top Rank Suite, the Locarno Ballroom, El Cubana and the Cat's Guest Night at the Seaburn Hall. It was great playing at the Locarno, situated on the Newcastle Road. It was actually spitting distance from the hospital where I had my wrist operated on. It was always full in those days. The dance floor, on a Wednesday night which was group night, would be packed. It had a balcony that came around each side of the stage where the girls would position themselves to eye up the boys on the floor and of course the groups!

There would always be several bands on during the group night. One of the highlights at the Locarno was it had a revolving stage. This was great, because it meant that the group waiting to come on could set up at the other side. Once the other band had finished, the next band would start playing as the stage rotated. It meant non- stop music all night. There was one downside to this however. The group's PA speakers had to be placed on the edge of the stage away from the revolving stage. This meant that as soon as the stage was in position, a member of the group on each side would be tasked with plugging in the lead to each speaker from the main amplifier. This was no problem until the end of the set. Playing·and getting carried away with the audience taking in the cheers and applause, the groups would very often forget to unplug the speakers as the stage started to move. The result was usually the big speaker cabinets being dragged to the floor with an almighty bang. As the stage moved reasonably fast, there was no way of rescuing them. It was then left to the roadie to go and rescue the speakers and hope they didn't find somebody underneath.

There was no doubt that although we were glad to be home, we were all missing the excitement of Germany. Why we would want to go back to playing 6 hours a night, staying in run down hotels and not getting paid very much seems crazy now. It had been the first taste of independence for us and being back home made us all feel like we had gone back to boys at home with their mums. We agreed to meet at Bob's house to discuss what we should do next. With mugs of tea and biscuits to hand, we all came tumbling out with our feelings. It was remarkable that we all felt the same. Well almost. Pete had seemed unhappy for some time and it came out that he was not happy with the band. It was a musical thing for him. Pete wanted to play more R&B type material and we were certainly strictly pop. We would play the odd Sam & Dave track like 'Hold on I'm Coming' but apart from that it was pop. There were bands around Sunderland like the Jazz Board who were dispensing good R&B and would also have a brass section. This added a dimension to the band that gave them credibility in this genre of music. Maybe because his father had played in a big band, Pete had an inkling to play with a brass section. He also said he didn't really want to go back to Germany, if that was what we wanted.

It was a shame to see Pete go, as we had got along with him well and he was a good guy and a good bass player. Pete and I had been close, so I was sorry to see him leave the band. I think drummers and bass players have an affinity, as they play closest together in any set up. We now had to find a bass player. Not only did we have to find one, we had to find one who also wanted to go to Germany.

We made a call to the German agent and said we would go as soon as he could get us some work. The feelers were out around the Sunderland circuit and one name came up that interested us. Arthur Webber. A meeting was arranged and in walked Arthur with his bass guitar. He fitted in immediately and he looked liked he had just walked out of the Small Faces. I also noticed he wore a long herringbone overcoat which he loved to wear all the time with a scarf. I thought that would be handy when driving to northern Germany in the middle of winter in a van with no heater. He played many songs with us in Bob's front room and it was obvious he was the man for the job. Now came the crunch. "Arthur, we would like you to join the group, but would you be willing to go to Germany"? The look on his face said it all. He had been waiting for this chance and the smile on his face said the cat had just got the cream. We were set, so all we had to do was wait for the phone to ring.

We finally got the call from the agent. We had been offered a month at The Star Palast in Lubeck for December 1966. We would then go to Hamburg to play The Funny Crow in January. Looking at the map, Lubeck was north of Hamburg, so the drive would be a long one and probably several degrees colder. Arnde was keen to get back to his native land too, so he was happy with the news. Bob's mum was also pleased, as she had not banked on having a lodger for quite so long. We were also up to date with our payments on the Vox amp so we were in credit for once. We now had a few weeks to prepare for our second tour and clubs were now billing us as 'Just before returning to the Top Ten Club' in Hamburg. Seeing the billing one night reminded us of the visit to the Funny Crow by Ricky Barnes from the Top Ten Club. As soon as we got to Germany, we told Arnde he must get in touch with him and see if we can get the booking we were promised.

Our parents were not exactly over the moon with the news that we would not be spending Christmas with them. The events that had taken place in Marburg had not been told in detail and something we definitely kept to ourselves. There was almost a group position that if we didn't talk about it, maybe it hadn't happened. One thing was for sure, we would not under any circumstances be going back there again. I still felt cold shivers of fear when I did think about that night. Winter in the North-East was setting in as we moved into November. Snow and ice were taking their toll on the roads as the icy wind would race over the North Sea to lash the faces of those daft enough to leave the comfort of their homes. That was constantly us, as we braved the A19 to places like Murton, where we would play at the Miner's Welfare or the various clubs that occupied the mining villages down the coast to

Middlesbrough and Stockton. The A19 was such a dangerous road then, as it was close to the sea and the wind would make the snow drift across the road. In the 60's, it was mainly single carriageway and was also very prone to thick fog. One thing had become apparent with our newly found transport as well – it did not have a heater! In those days, believe it or not, a heater was an 'optional extra' and this van was not big on extras. When we bought it, it was during the summer and it didn't make much difference. In fact, it was great to be driving along singing our hearts out with an acoustic guitar in the back with the sliding side doors wide open.

It struck me that the journey back to Germany was going to be tough. Not only did we not have a heater in the van, it was wintertime and we were about to drive to a place that was even further North than Sunderland on the global map. Preparation for the trip was minimal. Apart from having a float for petrol, we each had some money to get us food on the way there. Ferry tickets would be bought when we got to Dover. Entertainment would be courtesy of the little transistor radio which just about got a signal hanging from the driver's door handle. Completely useless to those of us who usually sat in the back.

Chapter Thirteen

The day arrived to depart for Germany for the second time. As the van pulled up outside our house in Ewesley Road, it was the end of November 1966 and bloody freezing. I wasn't sure whether the first time was best, knowing nothing of what was in store or now, when we knew what we were letting ourselves in for. It was also funny to see how the other guys were dressed. We all looked like Michelin Men, as we all had adorned vests, jumpers, woolly hats, sheep skin jackets, several pairs of socks and large scarves. The temperature had plunged to compound our misery, but we remained in good spirits. Winters in the North East of England in those days were legendary. Even the seagulls wore sheepskin jackets! We drove on to Hartlepool to pick up Malcolm and then off on the A1 for the South and later rather than sooner, Dover.

We had not gone long past Scotch Corner, when the van started to cough and judder before coming to a complete standstill. Arnde in his broken English was cursing the vehicle. 'This bloody bastard fucking English van is shit' was his first evaluation of the trouble. The engine was between the driver and passenger seat with a removable lid. This often acted as a seat when someone wanted to get a break from the back of the van. This was, of course, before the days of seat belt legislation. So, it was off with the cover and have a look at the trouble. Thankfully Arnde had a torch and we gave the engine a turn over. It was obvious petrol was not getting through to the engine. In the close confines of the cabin and nothing better than a torch light, the carburettor was dismantled. In the well of the carburettor were several pieces of 'gunk' which were coming up from the petrol tank and blocking the feed. It was obvious that the tank was rotten and this was a problem that was not going to go away. Having cleaned out the carburettor, it was reassembled and the van started first time of asking. Well, we were only 50 miles into a 1000-mile journey and already we were in trouble. Here we go again.

This was to be the situation for the rest of the journey. Every 100 miles or so, the van would splutter, we would pull in and clean out the carburettor and set off again. By the time we got to Dover, we had got the time of the job down to a few minutes. The port of Dover had grey skies over head and a chilling wind as we joined the queue of vehicles waiting to embark onto the ferry. As usual, there were plenty of group vans waiting to board and we walked down the line having a chat with them all, asking them where they were going. It was amazing how many there were. They were going to Germany, Holland and even as far as Italy by road. It was also alarming to see that most of the vans were no better than ours. Some were so over laden that the chassis was almost against the wheel arches. Goodness knows what the effect of hitting a bump in the road would do to it.

To the sound of the seagulls crying overhead, we slowly drove onto the ferry, hoping upon hope that the van would not splutter and spoil our chance of a place on board. We drove on at last and made our way up to the deck. Watching the White Cliffs of Dover disappear into the distance was always for me a sobering experience. Talking of sobering experiences – 'Did anyone fancy a beer?' It was into the bar and we had a pleasant crossing despite it being bitterly cold. The warmth of the bar on board the ferry was a welcome respite from the frozen box of the van.

As we drove off the ferry, we said our goodbyes to the other groups and wished them well. Our little van made its way through Calais for the long drive to Lubeck. It seemed to take much longer this time and it felt like years since we had been here before. I suppose so much had happened in that short few months. The road and the places rolled on through the night. Looking through the windscreen from our perches in the back of the van, the autobahn signs for Brugge, Antwerp, Eindhoven, Essen, Munster, Osnabruck, Bremen and Hamburg flashed by, illuminated by the van's headlights. Finally, and not before time, we drove into Lübeck. Lübeck is the largest German port on the Baltic Sea and situated on the Trave River. We were soon to discover that the club was down by the river and quite rough at night. It was where all the sailors would congregate to go drinking in the evening and fights and trouble were common place. Was this out of the frying pan back into the fire?

We also discovered that the RAF had made mince meat of the place during World War II and unfortunately in 1945 had bombed three ships in the harbour. These ships contained concentration camp inmates killing 7000 people on board. There had also been a POW camp called Oflag X-C which had housed several hundred allied POW's, so the place had a jolly history.

We were understandably tired and ready for some food. We also wanted to check out the club and see what it was like. Arnde was a god send, speaking the language, he found the club in no time. Being by the river made it feel very cold, but the club was OK and at least a good size. We met the owner who was getting his staff ready for the evening. Tables were being set as we went to check the stage. We were not due to play until the following night so we would have a chance for once to see what the club was like from the other side of the stage. The manager told Arnde where we were staying and we were pleased to hear that it was just a few blocks up from the club. We could not get our gear into the club until the following day so we drove up the road to the hotel. Well, hotel was something of a compliment. It was more like an old pub with a few bedrooms up the stairs. We were in a room at the front of the building overlooking the river. There were bunk beds in the room and the heating for the room as a little stove. As we were to discover, we would get one small bucket of coal per day to keep us warm. I wasn't sure whether we would light the fire or start to build an escape tunnel under the heater.

I was sure the old lady who showed us to the room was going to say, 'For you boys, the war is over'. Oh well, let's hope the club would be OK. We strolled off into the town to find somewhere to eat. Arnde was a good bet for this, as he loved his food. He couldn't wait to get his chops round a bratwurst with a mountain of sauerkraut. We found somewhere reasonably close and settled for burger and chips. I thought Arnde was going to have an orgasm as the final morsel of his heaped plate slithered down his throat, washed down with a stein full of frothy lager.

We decided to go straight to the club and avoid the Lübeck Hilton. That would certainly be somewhere for sleeping only. The club was already quite busy when we arrived around 7pm and the first band were already playing their first set. We settled into a booth at the back of the club and enjoyed the evening. The groups playing that night would come and join us when they had their break. One of the bands was from Poland called The Polanie. They were great fun and were mad. They warned us that the manager had a scam to deduct money from the band's earnings. In the contracts we signed for the engagement, which were in German with no English translation, there was a clause to say we were not allowed to smoke on stage. That was something we never did anyway, as we considered it to be unprofessional.

However, as they pointed out to us, he would get two waiters to say they had seen the band smoking and they would be fined accordingly. Well, we filed that one away for the future and would have to be on our guard. The Polanie were very good musicians. Their image was a little old fashioned, but we had such fun with them that night. They had us in stitches, as they could not say 'Arthur' as the letters 'th' do not feature together in their language. Like the German, he would be called 'Artur'. They were determined to pronounce his name and the more they tried the funnier it got. In the end, the only way they could say it properly was to hold their tongues and then say the word. We were crying with laughter and the locals must have wondered who they had got to entertain them for the coming month. For some strange reason The Polanie had started their month in the middle of November so we were to spend two weeks with them before they left for Warsaw.

We slept well that night despite the cold and soon discovered the bucket of coal did not go very far. We had invested in the individual electrical elements you stuck in mugs to boil water to make tea. These were a valuable tool and lifesavers in keeping you from suffering from hypothermia. We had bought some bread and cheese to give us some breakfast and by mid morning we were off to load the gear into the club. I noticed the waiters eyeing us up and I said to Malcolm not to forget to keep his cigarettes, as well as everything else, in is pocket.

We had a good sound check and the club had a nice warm sound which always helps. Some clubs can have terrible acoustics, which no matter how good you are can make a band sound tinny. The Polanie were staying at another place, which was probably just as well, as I reckon they would have wrecked the place we were in. Coming down the stairs, we had to walk through the bar to get out. Every time we came down the stairs, it seemed that the same dozen people were sitting in the same places. They just looked at us without saying anything and the old woman, who ran the place, just nodded as we went off into the night. Thank goodness, we were musicians and not RAF pilots!

We were pleased to strike up our first notes back in Germany and we got off to a flying start rocking the place all night. Our earlier experience in Germany and our big repertoire was now paying off. We were really enjoying playing and the harmonies and playing reflected that. Arthur had fitted in very well and was certainly finding Germany an experience. The first two weeks were nearly up and The Polanie were due to leave in a couple of days. The drummer from the Polanie, Piotrek, had warned us earlier we should be careful at night when we finished at the club. They had had some problems with sailors, who got very drunk and wanted to fight everybody. Apparently, they got very aggressive if they found out you weren't German. We had taken his advice and we all left together every night. He showed me a gas gun he had bought for his protection and asked me if I wanted to buy it. He couldn't take it back to Warsaw, as he was worried it would be found when they went through customs. I bought it for five deutsche marks and he gave me a summary on how to fire it. It had explosive capsules that fired tear gas, so you could not kill anyone. It would give them a big shock, as it made a loud bang and covered them in tear gas. I took the gun and spare capsules and quietly pocketed them for later. On their last night, we had a really good evening and even joined them on stage when they were playing, which the crowd loved.

We certainly consumed a few beers that night, but managed to stay sober enough to finish the night without any problems. Of course, the following night we were confronted by the manager who informed us that two of his waiters had seen us smoking on stage and would be fining us 50 DM each for this misdemeanour. Arnde went ballistic. I guess the manager had not been used to English groups having a German roadie and he sounded off in German while we just stood there bemused. In the end, he decided to abandon that tactic, as Arnde had said he would get enough witnesses from friends we had made, who were regular customers in the club, to say we hadn't smoked on stage. Having been warned, we knew this was just a shameful ploy to get away with paying us our full fee. The Star Palast at Kiel also had the same reputation for doing the same thing. Word spread on the group jungle drums when it came to dirty tricks by club owners.

As the month ticked by, it would soon be Christmas. We were told that the club would be closed only on Christmas day, but would remain open for the rest of the time. This was not good news for us. We would rather the club remained open, as we would have to spend Christmas day in the Lübeck Hilton with the old cronies. Arnde did some checking around town and he found out that pretty much everything would be closed on Christmas Day, so we couldn't even go out anywhere to have a meal. Christmas Day arrived and after sleeping late, we all sat around on our bunks wishing everyone a happy Christmas. There were no presents, no cards, no coal and not much food. This was to be the worst Christmas I had ever spent. It was depressing to say the least. We decided that we would go into town and have walk around. At least we could see the Christmas lights in the centre of town and hope upon hope we could find somewhere open. We didn't find anywhere and the thought of everyone at home tucking into turkey and Christmas pudding was the final straw. We eventually got back to the hotel and for once, sat in the bar with the wild bunch and had a few beers.

I think we were in bed by 9pm and couldn't wait for the day to end. As we went off to bed, the old woman must have taken pity on us because she gave us an extra bucket of coal. I didn't know whether to eat it or burn it. We thanked her for her kindness and trundled up to our room. Happy Christmas everyone, lights out. The next morning, we were up early and off up the road to get some decent food. Even the bratwurst looked good. We stuffed ourselves with chips and sausage, eggs, burgers and gallons of coffee. Now we were back in business and at least the club and most of the town would be open again.

Back on stage with everyone back to normal was heaven for us. If they had only known how bad a day we had had, I am sure someone would have offered us some hospitality. As we finished for the night, we split up as we were pursuing some of the local girls. It was time for some company. Our time for loneliness had to be put to an end. Unfortunately, none of us scored that night and by the time our efforts were in vain, I looked around and realised the boys had already left the club. I said my good byes at the club entrance and wandered off up the road by the river back to the hotel.

The sky overhead was very dark, with almost no moon and street lighting was almost non-existent. I had only got about two blocks from the club when out of the shadows lurched a large figure. He was wearing a navy-blue trench jacket and the black peaked cap, so much favoured by German sailors. His voice was very low and guttural and it was obvious he had had a few to drink. He lurched towards me as my mind was racing. I started to calculate all the factors. He was big, I wasn't. I was sober by now and he wasn't. Could I out run him? This was possible, but not certain. I also wondered if I could get straight into the hotel or would the outer door be locked? If that was the case he would catch up and I would be no better off. Then the blade flashed in his hand. 'Kompt hier Englischer'. Having faced what seemed like certain death in Marburg, twice in one year was getting to be too much of a habit. I was terrified now. It was very dark and there was not another soul around.

I remember hearing the creaking of the boats that were tied up along the river, straining on their ropes as the river made its way to the Baltic. The way things were going, I might be joining it. I had to remain calm. He was now moving in on me. I tried speaking to him and asking, 'What did he want with me'? I tried 'I am only a musician, why do you want to hurt me'? It did not seem to make any difference. It must have been my fear, but he seemed to be getting taller by the minute. Maybe I was shrinking, trying to be invisible. It was then I felt the bulge in my jacket pocket. It was the gas gun. I had not fired it before, so I did not know what would happen. This was no time to be squeamish. I took the gun out of my pocket and pointed it at him. He suddenly stopped in his tracks. I was trying hard not to shake and remember this was no Clint Eastwood movie, this was bloody real. He must have seen the gun, even though it was dark because his mood changed dramatically. I was now only interested in getting out of there. I didn't have some clever script to shout at him before finishing him off. Suddenly in a flash he came at me and I squeezed the trigger. The bang was enormous and it was followed by a spurt of gas that seemed to engulf him. He screamed and tried to cover his eyes. This was my chance and I just ran in the direction of the club as fast as I could.

At first, I wasn't certain where I was going, I just wanted to get away. The survival instinct took over and I got my bearings and headed for the hotel. Thankfully the door was open and there sat the old woman with her mates. Were they frozen in time? It seemed like they had never moved. It must have been around 3am. As usual she nodded and I sprinted up the stairs and made straight for the toilet where I threw up. When I got to the room, the boys were almost asleep. I was covered in cold sweat. They soon came around when I started to relate the tale; I was jabbering twenty words to the dozen. Out came the tea makers and after a cup of hot sweet tea, I eventually started to calm down. They thought it was hilarious and wanted to know every detail of how the gun worked and whether we should go and see if he was still there. I said they must be crazy and I wasn't leaving the room until there was daylight. Even then I would not be going alone. I tried to get to sleep but I kept seeing the image of this navy-blue trench coat and the blade coming at me in the dark. Finally, out of sheer exhaustion, I fell into a deep but troubled sleep.

The following day after a late breakfast, we ventured out and walked down to where I was sure the incident had happened. There was certainly no sailor there now, and I was just hoping whoever it was had set sail and left for good. Of course, the boys kept coming up behind me and giving me frights. With a large diet of German food and scares like that, I was certainly never going to be constipated. A couple of nights later while we were playing, we saw coming into the club four girls whom we had got to know at the Funny Crow in Hamburg. They had taken the train and come up to see us which was great. At last we had something to cheer us up. They were great girls and wanted to stay the night, as the last train left long before they wanted to leave. I expect they thought they could stay with us, believing that we were in some nice hotel! Unfortunately, we would never get them past the welcome committee and climbing up walls and drainpipes was out of the question. The only alternative was the van. We felt duty bound to keep the girls company as they had made the effort to come and see us. With the help of various blankets and sheepskin jackets we made the most of a very uncomfortable situation. The temperature was plummeting and with no heat it was not the best. It didn't take long before much shuffling, groaning and heavy breathing overtook the silence and before long the van was rocking from side to side as we did our best to keep each other warm.

In the morning we were all very stiff and uncomfortable, but the extra activity had been good compensation. We walked the girls into town and had a welcome coffee before dropping them off at the railway station. After that, the month seemed to fly by and apart from Christmas Day and my fun by the river, had been a good month. Arnde had managed to phone the Top Ten Club and spoken to Ricky Barnes to tell him we were in Germany if he wanted to book us. As it happened, he had just had a group drop out for February and would we like to do it. Well, we didn't have to think twice. A chance to play at the famous Top Ten Club was too good to miss and it was an emphatic 'Yes please'. We were booked to play back at the Funny Crow in January and after completing our month in Lübeck, we checked out of the 'Hilton', said our goodbyes to the old woman and headed south for Hamburg.

Chapter Fourteen

The weather was still freezing cold and being so far north, it did not help our cause having a van with no heater. We took to removing the lid off the engine between the driver and passenger seat and trying to get some warmth off the engine block. We were getting quite used to Hamburg now, and it was like going home, as far as Germany was concerned. As we had spent quite a bit of time there, we knew our way around town much better than any other German town we had been to. We were back in the same hotel and in the same basement we had been in before. As soon as we got there, it was off to the Dsching Gao for a Chinese meal and some good old special fried rice.

During the first week we were back at the Funny Crow, Helga Boddin from NDR's 'Twen Club' was back at the club and she booked us again for the 14th January 1967 with Lee Curtis and the All Stars. They were from Liverpool and had a big following in Germany. The show was recorded early evening, so we had to ask Alex again if it was OK to start a little later than usual. He was delighted because most of his customers went to the recording and would all come to the club after it finished anyway. He also knew it would be good for business if our following increased after the broadcast.

The day came and we loaded our gear in the van for the short drive to the radio studios. It as the same studio as before, so we were not so nervous this time knowing we had done OK. Unbelievably, we performed ten songs and Lee Curtis did twelve. It was quite a big session for us, but we ran through the numbers and the songs sounded good. The songs we did on the show reflected a cross section of our repertoire and were as follows:

Midnight Hour – Wilson Pickett /Get Out of My Life Woman – Lee Dorsey

Hey Little Girl – The Syndicate of Sound / Land of 1000 Dances – Lee Dorsey

You Go Too Fast For Me – self penned by myself and Bob / Gimme Some Lovin' – Spencer Davies Group / Take This Hammer – traditional / Semi Detached Suburban Mr. Jones – Manfred Mann / Bend It – Dave Dee etc / High Time Baby – Spencer Davis Group / Sorry She's Mine – Small Faces

It was a great experience again and we had a good chat with Lee Curtis and his band after the recording. We didn't have long, as we had to get the gear back to the Funny Crow for our night's labours. We were on a great high and once again, so many of the Funny Crow crowd were in the audience. They had given us a fantastic cheer and applause every time we had performed a number. So, it was all back to the club and let's do it all again. The other good thing was that we got a nice fee for the gig, so we had a bit of spare cash for once. This was a rarity for us and it made a difference having some proper cash in the pocket. Of course, with our luck it didn't last long. Arnde informed us that the van needed some attention as the engine was playing up and needed a good service. The bill came to DM354.90 which was a big amount in 1967 with a currency rate of 10DM to the pound. What God gives he surely takes away and our radio bonus went straight back into the van. Bollocks!

During one of the evenings during the month we were chatting to Alex during a break and he asked us where we were playing next. His face changed from cordiality to rage, when we told him we were at the Top Ten Club. He said we were not allowed to play there according to our contract. We were shocked and devastated that our chance to play one of Hamburg's premier venues was about to slip through our grasp. He informed us that in our contract, which none of us had read, it barred us from playing another club in Hamburg for three months after playing at the Funny Crow. We tried to reason with him but he was a hard business man and wouldn't budge. Now we were confused and angry. How could he be so unreasonable after all we had done for him? We filled his club every night and the Top Ten was in the centre of town on the Reeperbahn and his club was in the suburb of Grindelberg. He insisted that if we played there, his entire crowd would go and see us and he would lose money. We knew a few would come on odd nights, but it was a completely different crowd that frequented the Top Ten and Star Club. In any case, the club crowd used to visit all the clubs during a night, so we didn't see why he was making such a fuss.

Now we were torn between our big chance and upsetting a regular booking. We sat and talked back at the hotel into the early hours of the morning. We finally decided that it was too good a chance to miss and we could finally prove ourselves. Alex was being unreasonable and he lost a lot of respect from us for that. For the rest of the month we did not discuss anything with him and when we left, he was not there as usual to say goodbye. It was a sad end to our time at the Funny Crow and as we drove off to the Top Ten we were hopeful that he would cool off and reconsider his position.

The Top Club was situated right in the middle of the Reeperbahn in the St. Pauli area of Hamburg. This was the centre of the sex trade in the city and block after block there were sex clubs on either side of the road. This was a long way from Ewesley Road Methodist Church! The small roads leading off the Reeperbahn also housed lots of sex clubs and on one of these side roads, the Grosse Freiheit, just around the corner from the Top Ten was the famous Star Club. The Reeperbahn was quite a big wide road and very long. We managed to park outside the entrance and started the load in. This was very exciting for us and it was like walking into rock history. We were all aware of the Beatles and their previous history both hear and at the Star Club.

We were to share the month with an Irish Show band. The Germans loved bands that could 'mach show' and these Irish guys were as mad as hatters and would throw themselves all over the stage. They had a big line up with two singers and a big brass section so, compared to just the four of us, we seemed tiny by comparison. Each drummer set up at the back of the stage either stage left or right and each band set their back line in front of the drum risers. As we had seen earlier, the Top Ten had its own PA system and mikes, so that solved one problem when sharing with another band. When you entered the club from the street, about half way down the corridor leading to the club was a door. Through that door was a staircase leading upstairs to where the groups had their own accommodation. It was very basic fair and each room was stacked with bunk beds. It had all the finesse of a school dormitory in a bad school. Still, with the hours we were to be playing it would not matter. The Irish band had certainly collared all the best rooms and we ended up in one room with two bunks. Everyone suddenly developed vertigo and didn't want the top bunk. After a spin of the coin, that was soon sorted and we waited with anticipation for our first night at the famous club.

It came quickly enough and before long we were on stage straight into our first number. Being right in the heart of town, the club was already quite full and by 9am it was heaving. The club would continue to be packed out all night every night. We would play one hour on stage then have a one-hour break while the show band played. If we started at 7pm we finished at 5am and if we started at 8pm we finished at 6am. Weekends we started an hour earlier. There were nights, when I felt my drum stool had been welded to my arse it was so sore. We quickly got to know all the hookers, who used to come in to the club to see the bands and have a break from their nightly toils. They were good to the boys in the band. They knew we all didn't have much money and would regularly buy us drinks. They were the epitome of 'tarts with a heart'. I had never encountered prostitutes before and my perception of them changed significantly after that. They were kind, funny and protective of their boys and they never mixed business with pleasure!

The Top Ten and Star Club also had their own groupies. I guess these clubs had a certain status and therefore the bands who played there inherited status as well. The groupies all seemed to specialise. Some wanted only the lead singer, bass player, guitarist or drummer. Girls were supposed to be out of bounds up stairs in our accommodation and frankly no one was keen to take anyone up there. It was so crowded; you might as well have had sex in the middle of the club. Ricky Barnes would hang around the back of the club where the waiters would collect their drinks orders. He would keep a watchful eye on the bands, making sure they were playing properly and not messing around.

In the early hours of the morning we would occasionally swop instruments just to make a change. When we were playing for so long, it helped just for one number to enable us to do something different. Booker T & the MGs track 'Green Onions' was always a favourite although we would keep it short as Ricky was alert to what we were up to. One morning, after climbing into bed and sinking into a deep sleep, Ricky came knocking on our door after a couple of hours. The Top Ten was also a recording studio and during the day they converted it. Around the dance floor were sockets where mikes could be plugged into and a glass window to the side, hidden by a curtain, could be drawn back to reveal the control room. They were doing a session with Tony Sheridan and the bass player had not turned up. They dragged Arthur down to do the session and we dropped off back to sleep. Poor Arthur could hardly stand, let alone play the bass, and he couldn't even remember what he had played. However, he was certainly glad of the session fee he got for his trouble.

Despite the hard work, we were really enjoying the month and being in the centre of things. We had been sent some records that had charted in the UK so we could learn some more new tunes. We now had a repertoire of over sixty songs which was a record for us. One of the records sent was a track by an unknown American guitarist called Jimi Hendrix. We soon learnt 'Hey Joe' and loved the earthy sound the band had captured on record. It was like nothing else around at the time. We also heard that Hendrix was going to play a one-night stand at the Star Club during the month we were at the Top Ten. With a bit of luck, we might get to see him. A couple of nights later, I noticed a few people coming into the club and being greeted by Ricky. One of the group had a big afro hair cut and was wearing an old-fashioned military style jacket with lots of gold braid. I recognised Chas Chandler from the Animals, who was managing them and the others turned out to be Noel Redding and Mitch Mitchell (The Experience). They made their way to a table which was virtually next to me on the drums. The military man turned out to be Hendrix who was smoking the biggest spliff I had ever seen. He was with a blonde German girl whose breasts seemed to match the proportion of his spliff.

Jimi was obviously into 'big'. Amongst this entourage was the jazz trumpeter Chris Barber. Apparently, they had met Chris on the Reeperbahn and invited him to join them for a drink. After our set, we went over to have a chat with them. We at least could converse with Chas, as he came from Newcastle. We all got on well and they invited us to their Star Club gig. Jimi was to be on stage at midnight. As luck would have it, we were due to be off between midnight and 1am. They arranged for our names to be on the door and as soon as we finished at 11.59pm we ran out of the club, down the Reeperbahn and into the Grosse Freiheit. Thankfully they were as good as their word and our names were on the door. We literally only just got through the door as it was packed. The Star Club was a converted cinema, so it had the shape of a theatre, much longer in size than the Top Ten. Before long they were on stage and going through their set. This was mind blowing for us to see Jimi perform. Up until then it had all been suits, harmonies and pop. Suddenly this right-handed Fender Stratocaster guitar strung left handed was singing out across the club. Then he was playing it with his teeth. It was hard to take it all in and no sooner had we got there, then we had to ease our way out of the crowd and head back to the Top Ten to do our next set at 1am. We all felt like Cinderella that night and wished we could have seen the end of the show. Apparently, he set fire to his guitar and then shoved it into the ceiling above the stage.

The rest of the night we were on a high and must have played 'Hey Joe' several times to an eager crowd. Our sets got a bit harder edged from that night onwards. We also saw a band at the Star Club called the Kingpins and they featured a track in their set called 'Hey Little Girl' by an American band called The Syndicate of Sound. It was a great number and we managed to get a copy of the record to add it to our repertoire. It was a high paced number and suited our style down to the ground. It was a great 'Hamburg' number and seeing it work in the Star Club was enough for us. It certainly rocked the aisles in the Top Ten as well.

Some nights later, I noticed a nice blonde girl taking a lot of interest in me. At the end of the set, she waved me over and bought me a beer. She was wearing a nice green outfit that seem to give her certain sophistication. She looked stunning. We got on well and her name was Karen. We continued to chat through our break and she was great company. I was back on stage for another hour and she remained at the table, dancing occasionally with her friends. I joined her at each break and it looked like I was doing well here. My heart as racing and she had a fantastic figure to go with her good looks. As we came off after the last set, she remained at the table and without any conversation, she took my hand and we were out on the Reeperbahn. We walked up a few blocks and stopped in front of hotel. It was one of those hotels which had a single door leading onto the street. You went through the door and immediately up a set of stairs to reception and the rooms on the first floor. She opened the door with her key and we climbed the stairs, through a corridor and into her room.

The room overlooked the Reeperbahn and the window was open as it was a hot summer's night. The traffic and the sounds of revellers filtered up through the window as she took off her jacket and threw it on the chair. I noticed a copy of the Daily Mirror on the table, which seemed an odd read for a German girl. She put her arms round me and shoved me onto the bed. We lay next to each other and started kissing. Gradually, pieces of our clothing ended up on the floor until we were completely naked. She looked divine. We snuggled up under the duvet and by now I was on the Cresta Run and about to hit 100 mph. Just then, the sound of music from a vehicle drifted up through the open window and voices accompanying the slamming of van doors.

She immediately jumped out of the bed and ran to the window. 'Shit, you've got to go now' as her voice intoned a certain amount of panic. By now I'm out of the bed and scrambling around looking for my clothes. 'It's my husband; he was supposed to be staying away tonight. They must have changed their minds and come back'. Whilst dragging on my trousers, the thought of being beaten to a pulp by a jealous husband was not going down too well. My night of passion had come to a sudden and dramatic end. With trousers and shirt on, I grab the rest of my gear and out into the corridor. I hadn't got a clue where I was or where to go. I could hear the keys in the front door to the street, so I ran down the corridor and around the corner out of sight. I could hear my heart pumping and my stomach churning. This was Hamburg and violence was always just around the corner. Seeing the body of a prostitute in a side street after being shot by her pimp a couple of days earlier had not made my nerves settle one little bit. The corridor was a dead end and there were only the doors of various rooms and no exit. The only way out was back up the corridor and passed her room.

I could hear footsteps coming up the stairs and the door of her room opened and closed. By now, I was fully dressed but felt naked. I started to quietly make my way back down the corridor, slip passed her room door and down the stairs to make my escape. Wrong! Fuck, the door to the street was locked and it was not a latch type lock but a mortise lock. This was now turning into a bloody nightmare. What the hell was I going to do? I couldn't go and knock on her door and as it was in the early hours of the morning, it was unlikely anyone was going to turn up and let themselves in (and me out)! Just then the manager appeared from reception and started berating me in German. I could pick up a couple of words, but it didn't take a linguist to work out he is not happy by my presence. He obviously thought I had somehow broken into his hotel. I pick up the word 'politzei' and that scares the life out of me. I had already pictured me being deported or even worse. Karen had obviously heard the commotion from inside her room and stuck her head round the door. She quickly spoke to the manager and whatever she said seemed to appease him. He eventually came down the stairs with the key. With a begrudging nod and a 'Thank You' from me, I was out into the Reeperbahn and legging it back to the digs above the Top Ten Club. The boys think it is hilarious but I certainly didn't share the joke. It was not a nice thought being caught in bed with somebody else's wife. Still, as I drifted off to sleep, I couldn't help but wonder about the delights of Karen and how close I had been to finding out. We weren't angels, but we did have our own code of honour. The following day, I was sorting out the van, which was parked outside the Top Ten, when along comes Karen as if everything was fine. She apologises for the previous night. It turned out her husband was English and played drums with Lee Curtis's All Stars. That explained the Daily Mirror in the room. I remembered him from the radio show we had done with them which made me feel even worse.

She was still very keen and wanted me to go back to see her that night. As much as I fancied her like hell, I couldn't bring myself to be with her knowing she was married. I also had no intention of going back to that hotel either. Getting stuck in a hotel corridor after being in bed with another man's wife might be funny in a Brian Rix play; the reality in the sex capital of the world was somewhat different. She came to the club that night and bought me drinks, but I still would not oblige. As the night ended, I saw her leave the club with another guy and thought how sad it was. I often wondered how long their marriage would last. I guess she thought her old man was shagging everything in sight when he was away so why shouldn't she?

Chapter Fifteen

One afternoon, we decided to have a walk up the Reeperbahn to have a look round the shops and a cheeky nose at the sex shops. We finally ended up in Music City. We would often go and visit this shop during the day for something to do. It was also a chance to keep up with the latest gadgets that were being introduced. I was aware that my hi-hat cymbals were poor and the sound they generated not quite up to scratch. I had been saving up some money over the previous weeks and on this visit, found a lovely pair of Zyldjian hi-hat cymbals. They weren't cheap, but I just had to have them. I shelled out the DM200 and they were mine. It is hard to explain to someone who hasn't played an instrument what it is like to get a new guitar or drum. When you are performing regularly you often needed something new to stimulate your interest. My old hi-hats sounded like dustbin lids by comparison and the new shiny ones sounded crisp, light and looked incredibly shiny. That night, I was in my element and it gave the kit a new lease of life, not least me. The Irish Show Band were leaping about the stage as usual and I watched anxiously as they came close to smashing into my kit with their antics.

Ricky Barnes was originally from Scotland and he was a decent saxophone player. When the mood took him, he would wander from the back of the club and come on stage and play along with us for a couple of numbers. The entire crowd new him and he used to get a great reception from them. The month went very quickly from then on and we were booked to play in a club in Dusseldorf the following month. We had not been that far south before, so it was a new adventure and we were looking forward to seeing a new German city. The time at the Top Ten had been a great experience and I think we all grew up a lot during that month. Whereas the Funny Crow had been a 'safe' gig, we had to prove ourselves at the Top Ten Club. It had its reputation and been home to some great bands. As it happened, we were destined never to return to Hamburg again. On our final night, we played our hearts out and had a party with the Irish show band before grabbing a couple of hours sleep. It was an easy load out of the club that morning and after we were all packed, our Austin van chugged down the Reeperbahn for the last time and onto the autobahn south.

The 400-kilometre journey took us around five hours and we drove into Dusseldorf late afternoon. After a couple of stops to ask directions, we soon found the club. It was situated on Graf Adolf Strasse and called The Liverpool Club. It was a similar size to the club in Marburg and the stage ran along the back wall with the bar down the left-hand side of the club. It looked OK but didn't have the cool reputation of the Top Ten Club, so it felt like we had gone back to a lower division. The load in did not take long and after a quick sound check; it was off to the hotel where the owner had arranged our accommodation. Once again, we were all in one big family room, but it was clean and comfortable, so we were happy enough.

We noticed on the first night we played that there were quite a few English people in the club. During our breaks, they would happily buy us drinks and want to know where we had come from and where we lived in England. They were mostly army people, as there was a massive army base at Rheindalen. This had been established at the end of World War 2 and although we didn't know it then, it was to be our saviour later. It was during one of our late-night sets that we noticed a couple come into the club. It was obvious that they were well known and it looked like they were treated like VIPs. The girl was blonde and very attractive and the guy she was with was well dressed in a velvet jacket no less. They were immediately shown to a table at the front of the club and right in front of the stage. They were certainly taking note of all of us and seemed to be assessing each of us in turn. We were rattling out a good set and our harmonies were spot on. The 'Hamburg Throats' were as hard as nails by now and we could sing for hours. We had now included Purple Haze by Hendrix into our set and we ended off with a stomping version just before 10pm. As soon as we left the stage the manager came over and said we had been invited over to the table at the front for a drink. We were certainly intrigued. The guy with the velvet jacket stood up and introduced himself. "Hi guys, I'm Casey Jones and this is Renate". The devil in me wanted to say "Hello Casey, where's your fucking train engine? For once, tact took over and we all meekly said 'Hello'.

Casey, real name Brian Casser, had formed a group in Liverpool called Cass and the Casanova's, which had in turn become the Big Three. The original members ousted Casey. He then moved to London in 1961 and managed a club called The Blue Gardenia in Soho. In 1963, when the Liverpool scene had exploded, Casey formed another band called Casey Jones and the Engineers. They had little success in the UK and moved to Germany where they changed their name to Casey Jones and the Governors. They recorded a single called 'Don't Ha Ha' which sold a million copies in Germany. We had heard of the band and the name was familiar, but our knowledge of him was limited.

It turned out that the Governors had left him, recorded a version of the Mindbenders 'Groovy Kind of Love' and were enjoying success in their own right as opposed to being his backing group. He bought us a couple of beers and said he was looking for a new backing group, were we interested? This was a new twist to our careers and something completely unexpected. We had never considered backing anyone and we said we would discuss his offer. He agreed to return the following evening for our answer. Back at the hotel we burned the midnight oil discussing our options. As it happened, we had nothing lined up for the following month and it was looking likely that we would return to the UK. After much soul searching, we decided to accept his offer. It would be good to taste a bit of fame, even if it was as a backing group.

The following night Casey returned to the club and we confirmed we would accept his offer. He seemed pleased that he had sorted out his problem as he had dates coming up which had to be fulfilled. We set about learning 'Don't Ha Ha' and 'Jack the Ripper' which was a rip off of Screaming Lord Sutch's track. Casey would pull a stocking over his head and wear Dracula teeth to perform the song which was very cheesy, but the audience seemed to love it. He also told us that we could stay at his flat in Dusseldorf. We went over to check it out and it was one large room (again) with four single beds in it. We had to pay him rent, but he agreed that we would get paid DM100 each per gig. This was good money in 1967 and when we started with him we were playing three or four gigs a week.

Casey had his own road manager called Kurt and this left us with a problem with Arnde. Arnde was getting restless in any case, as most of his time was spent doing nothing, as we were resident in one place for a month at a time. He decided to head back home to Hamburg at the end of the month. It was sad parting with Arnde, as he had become a good friend. We had been through a lot together and not least the events in Marburg, where I am sure he saved our lives. The end of the month came and we said 'Goodbye' to Arnde as he headed for the railway station in Dusseldorf. Kurt picked up our gear and the following day we moved in with Casey and Renate. We still had the old Austin van which none of us could drive (legitimately) so for now it was parked outside the flat.

Chapter Sixteen

The first few months were good and it was exciting playing to big crowds in clubs and concert halls. As we had been in the country for longer than expected, we had to go and renew our work permits. We took our passports to the Foreign Workers office in Dusseldorf and found the entertainment section. They had a person in charge of issuing work permits to groups as there were so many in Germany at that time and he knew all the English bands very well. The building where the office was housed had a strange lift system. It was a set of lifts that permanently rotated and they did not have closing doors. You had to have the knack of jumping into it as it came level with the floor you were on and jumping off when you got to the floor you required. This was very scary and it took a fair number of attempts before we could actually ride up the lift. Of course, the people that worked there looked at us as if we were aliens, as they casually trotted on and off the hideous contraption. When we finally got into the office, the officer pulled our file from his draw and perused it with interest.

After reading through some notes, he announced he couldn't renew our permits. Alexander Zucker, owner of the Funny Crow in Hamburg had lodged court papers against us for breach of contract. So, he had issued a court action against us. We were horrified. It seemed incredibly mean for him to take such action. Whether we had played the Top Ten or not, it hadn't made the slightest difference to his business and we had made a packet for him getting the crowds into his club every night. We returned to the flat in Dusseldorf and told Casey the news. He was quite unfazed by this and said he would call his lawyer and get it fixed. The following day, his lawyer called and said he could pay off Alexander to withdraw the court papers and Casey agreed to stump up the money. A few days later we returned to the permit office and our work permits were duly renewed. The officer laughed as he stamped our passports and said we must have friends in high places.

Casey came into our room one day and said we had been asked to support The Who at the Rheinhalle in Dusseldorf. The Who had been our heroes for some time and we included a lot of their tracks in our repertoire. Now we had the chance to play with them. When the day came, we were buzzing and got to the hall in the afternoon for sound check. Keith Moon's massive red sparkling Premier Kit was already set up on a huge drum riser when we got there. Marshall stacks were in abundance and many a hairy roadie was running around with endless rolls of gaffa tape. We set up in front of their gear in the space left at the front of the stage; such was the life of support bands.

Backstage at The Who concert in Dusseldorf (L/R Casey Jones, Keith Moon, John Reed)

The only consolation was there was also a German band on before us and they had to set up in front of us! They had about two feet of space before they fell off the high stage. We were hanging around back stage when the Who arrived. It was amazing standing talking to them and Casey obviously knew them quite well. I sat and talked to Keith Moon who spent the whole time throwing whatever pills he could get hold of down his throat. He was a great 'larger than life' character and was constantly looking to cause mischief with whoever he felt looked like a victim. The German band went on at 7pm and warmed up the crowd. We were on at 8.00pm and went down quite well. The crowd knew Casey, as he was regarded as a local Dusseldorf boy. After our set we took the precaution of quickly moving all our gear to the very back of the stage behind some black curtains.

Sadly, the German band did not do the same and their gear was to be subsequently wrecked during My Generation. The Who were awesome and very loud. Hit after hit was belted out and Pete Townsend's power chords shook the very foundations of the hall. At the end of their show they went into 'My Generation' and at its climax Townsend swirled his Fender

Telecaster guitar around his head intending to impale it into the Marshall speakers. Unfortunately, he let go of the guitar too early and it went sailing into the audience. We watched from the side of the stage as the guitar flew heading for its final destination – the head of a guy sitting in the front stalls. Crack, the base of the guitar contacted the young fan and he went down in a pool of blood. The German equivalent of the St. John's Ambulance came running down the hall with a stretcher and carried him off to hospital. As they were trying to stem the flow of blood, one of the roadies stepped over them all to retrieve the offending guitar and had it back to Townshend who proceeded to smash it into the speaker cabinet. Drums, amps, guitars went flying. The poor German band were in tears as they could only stand and watch as their prized gear was smashed to pieces. We had a few beers with The Who after the show, but they quickly left for the airport as they wanted to be in the next city for their show the following day.

Backstage at the concert with The Who in Dusseldorf (L/R Casey Jones, Pete Townsend, John Reed)

For us, it was back to our flat in Dusseldorf and try and get some sleep, as the adrenalin was pumping after such a high energy night. Our next show, we were told, was to be at the Green Hell Club in Berlin two days later. It was a good six-hour drive and we had the hassle of going through the East German sector. This was always a nightmare, especially for a group of musicians with long hair. As usual, Kurt pulled in to the services at Magdeburg, the last autobahn services before entering the Eastern sector. We all had a beer and a sandwich before continuing towards Berlin. At the start of the sector, signs indicating that 'You are now leaving the American Sector' almost said 'if anything happens to you now folks, you are on your own so don't bother calling us'. The process of entering East Germany was long and tedious. There were about six check points you had to drive through, all covered in barbed wire and various car traps to stop anyone making a break for it. You also had to drive over a pit where guards would examine the undercarriage of the vehicle in case someone was hiding there. Each check point was manned by several armed guards, who all stared at you suspiciously, as they examined your passports.

They had all been indoctrinated and we were treated with contempt as Western capitalists. We had to buy a transit visa which was DM10 each for a return visa. Having not worked for a while we were not very flush with money, so we decided to just buy a one way visa for DM5 and get the other on the way back after being paid for the gig in Berlin. By the time we got through the check points and onto the autobahn for our onward journey to Berlin we were now feeling the effects of the beers we had drunk in Magdeburg. We got Kurt to stop on the side of the autobahn and we all rushed out of the van to relieve ourselves. After the initial feeling of relief, someone said 'Don't look now lads but we're being watched'. I looked up through the endless pine trees that seemed to dominate that part of the world and spotted a watch tower. The tower was manned by East German guards who were training a machine gun on us and eyeing us up with their binoculars. I have never felt less like a pee in all my life. We then spotted the sign 'Achtung Minen'. So, we were having a pee in a minefield as well. This made for an interesting walk back to the van trying to remember what steps we had taken to get where we were. To cap it all off, Kurt then took the wrong junction on the autobahn and we had to drive for several kilometres before we could turn around. This made us late at the check point at the end of the autobahn which would then let us enter the centre of Berlin.

Each vehicle entering the East sector was timed through, as they reckoned that anyone spending more time than was necessary was obviously helping the locals to escape. As soon as we got to the first check point, our passports were examined and we were immediately directed through a barrier to a building beyond the barbed wire fences. I did not like the way this was going. We were taken into the building to an office where two grey uniformed soldiers went through our passports once again. They started to question us as to why we had taken so long to come through. Kurt explained his mistake, which even sounded limp to us and we knew he was telling the truth. He wanted to know why we were going to Berlin, what we did, how much we made, what did we think of the political situation in Israel? It was early 1967, and trouble was brewing between Israel and her neighbours. It was to finally culminate in the six-day war. That was off the wall for us. We didn't even know what was going on in Dusseldorf, never mind Israel.

We were then searched, thankfully not strip searched, but we were given a thorough going over. More was to come. They then started on the van. We had to take every piece of equipment out and each item was searched. Speaker cabinets were opened, amplifiers opened. Heads were taken off my drums, so they could see inside. Every cable box, tool box, even the jack plugs on guitar leads were screwed off to check if anything was hidden in them. All the panelling on the doors was stripped off to see if there was anything hidden behind them. The van was driven over a special well so someone could go down and inspect the underneath with a torch. They even measured the van to check we hadn't welded extra bits on the back to accommodate a fleeing East German. Eventually they were satisfied we weren't trying to smuggle someone into the Western sector. Apparently, we were free to go.

That is after we had reassembled our van and the entire contents, which were strewn over a large area in bits. To say we were not amused was an understatement, but you have that hopeless feeling that you cannot do a damn thing, because they can do with you what they will. If you cried 'I am a British Citizen and I demand to speak to the British Consul immediately' you would no doubt disappear forever. We quietly put the gear back together, loaded the van and drove off slowly as their grey soulless eyes followed our every move.

The Green Hell was aptly named and we had to do a one hour set at midnight. It was a strange club and was obviously frequented by Berlin's underworld. We were staying in rooms above the club and there seemed to be all sorts of comings and goings throughout the night. After we had done our set, Casey suggested we go to the manager's office and get paid. That way, we could get a couple of beers before going to bed. We had to be up early to get back to Dusseldorf the following day. We entered the manager's office, a sallow looking figure with greasy black hair. Casey said he had come for his money. The manager opened a drawer on his desk and pulled out an automatic pistol. He placed it carefully on the desk. "Casey, I am not going to pay you, what have you got to say to that?" I could feel my heart pumping and looked around slowly to see if anyone else was smiling. No one was smiling. Casey, not a man to be underestimated, grabs the gun and points it at the manager. "Yes, you fucking well are going to pay us. Don't pull this shit on me". There was a heart stopping moment and I really didn't want to be a part of that moment or any of the coming moments. I just wanted a quiet life and drink a few beers, not get shot. Marburg was bad enough and now we were seeing more guns than a John Wayne movie. The moment passed and the manager slowly began to laugh. 'Casey, you make me laugh, you were always a feisty one. Here is your money and so let us have a drink together'. He got a bottle of schnapps from behind his desk and some glasses and poured us all a drink. The tension visibly softened and Casey put the gun down. One thing for sure was that I was not going to get much bloody sleep now staying in this place with a gun toting German and a mental singer. We went back to the club and stayed up until around 4am. I was looking over my shoulder all night and was glad when dawn broke through the window knowing we would be on our way soon.

Casey told us later that he had heard from other bands that had played there that the manager often tried that stroke to get out of paying the bands. The signs were already there that Casey was a little crazy. It was nice to be paid, and after breakfast we headed for the check point to start our journey back to civilisation. We pulled in to the office at the check point to get our return visas. What they had failed to tell us on the way in was that the visa office was shut on a Sunday, so we would have to go back and return the following day. We really did not want to spend another day in Berlin and Kurt made some enquiries as to whether there was somewhere else we could get these transit visas. We were then told that the only other office open on Sundays was at Schönefeld Airport.

The only problem was that Schönefeld Airport was in East Germany. This would mean driving deep into the East to get the visas. We all agreed we didn't want to stay in Berlin, so we set off for the infamous Berlin Wall. After making some enquiries, it transpired that we had to go through Check Point Charlie and Kurt had to take the van through another check point some miles down the road as he was a German citizen. We said goodbye to Kurt and hoped we would see him shortly. We then had to go through Checkpoint Charlie on foot. There was a museum on the British side which contained bullet ridden cars used in escapes and poignant photographs of failed escape attempts. This really cheered us up. We had to exchange a certain amount of money into East German currency, which of course, we couldn't change on the way back. Commie bastards and they call us capitalists! After much explaining as to why we really wanted to enter their shit hole of a country, we had the long lonely walk to the other side passed shells of buildings with the Wall looming over us as we entered East Germany. We noticed that we could not hear any birds singing, it was silent. Even our feathered friends were making a protest at this shameless division of a nation. After what seemed like an eternity, we saw the gray transit in the distance and knew Kurt was not far away.

With the feeling of constantly being watched, we headed off in the direction of the airport which was 18 km drive. We stopped a couple of times to ask further directions and when the locals realised we were English, they disappeared as quickly as they had appeared. Hot on their heels would be an armed soldier with a German shepherd dog asking us why we were speaking to the local people. With little help from anybody, we eventually found Schönefeld Airport. The place was as drab as public toilet, gray walls with little light and full of miserable people with nothing to look forward to. All the flights were to the communist block from Berlin as nothing went west. We found the visa office and a very hostile public employee. He obviously hated being there, being himself and he hated us for having the cheek to come all the way to spoil his Sunday. He took our passports and money and disappeared. I am sure he went home, as he didn't come back until three hours later. He went through a door and that was the last we saw of him for three hours. There was no one to call or speak to and we were ignored by everyone.

When he did return he took the money for the visas and almost threw the passports at us. Without a word, he turned on his heels and disappeared again. We were off out of that hole within seconds and back to the check point where we again had to split up and get back to the West. It had been some day and thankfully the return journey was uneventful. It was with some joy we pulled into the services at Magdeburg for a decent cup of coffee and a beer. When we got back to Dusseldorf we slept long and hard. We then went out and celebrated with a meal of chicken and chips from Wienerwald, a chain of fast food restaurants that did fantastic rotisserie chicken which had become a favourite.

Casey had been negotiating with his record company, Vogue International, to make another record. He had also wanted to record the single in the UK and not Germany. In what was to be a last chance effort, they agreed to his demands and a date was set for us to travel to London and record two songs. We were happy about this for two reasons. One, we would have a chance to get back to the UK and at least have some decent English food and second, it would be good to get into a recording studio again. We left Düsseldorf for Calais, our favourite place (not) and across the channel, into Dover and we were in London arriving early on a Sunday morning.

We had arranged to meet the record company representative in Soho and after what seemed an interminable time, he finally arrived. He took us to our hotel and outlined the recording schedule for the following day. We were to record in the CBS Studios in Bond Street. The session was to start at 10am and finish at 1.00pm. A large orchestra had been booked and the arrangements were done by Mike Mansfield. The main tune we were recording was a track called 'Mervyn Guy'. It was written by Guy Fletcher and Doug Flett who had had some chart success with some of their other songs. Having listened to the demo, I was sure this was not going to be one of them! I subsequently found out that 'Mervyn' was indeed Guy Fletcher's first name so he had named the song after himself.

We duly arrived the following day in Bond Street and the entrance to the studio was round a side street just off the main road. It was on the first floor so our gear had to be lugged up the stairs and into the reception area. When we arrived, we were able to get our gear into the studio but an all-night mixing session was over running in the control room. It was obvious that drums, bass, guitar and keyboards had already been booked as part of the orchestra. This did not go down too well with us. Why had we travelled all the way from bloody Germany just to watch some other bugger play on the record? We were hopping mad. A compromise was reached and we were set up along side the session musicians. I suspect that our contribution was very low in the final mix although it does sound like to drummers on the actual record.

We settled down outside the control room having coffees waiting for the other session to finish. It was only then that we started to take notice of the sounds coming from within. The haunting organ sound and distinctive vocal. One listen and it was obvious to anyone that this was a special record. It was the final mix down session for Procol Harem's 'Whiter Shade of Pale'. It was exhilarating on the one hand, but massively depressing on the other. To have to first listen to such a fantastic record was amazing, but then weighed up against 'Mervyn Guy', I wanted to throw myself under a London bus.

Eventually they vacated the studio and departed with what appeared to be a very smug look on their faces and who could blame them? The session musicians had assembled and there was a full orchestra. Rhythm section, brass and string sections were everywhere inside the full studio. I took my seat on the kit next to the session drummer who told me not to worry, he would guide me through. Having an MD standing in the middle of the studio with a baton was scary stuff and I was trembling in case I fluffed my part. Having all those musicians staring at me, especially if they had to do their piece again because of some hairy drummer. My nerves were in pieces and I felt physically sick. I was beginning to wish I had not made a fuss and just let the session musicians do their thing. We did our first run through and I got through it OK. It finally came to do a 'record' and the red light was on. One, two, three, four – we were in. It was great fun playing with such great players and I now had to be careful not to get too carried away and start speeding up the tempo. This is one of the common faults of live drummers and session guys were like metronomes. After two takes the producer was happy and my lower intestine could finally relax. We went into the control room to hear the play back and were happy with the result.

After we had done the 'B' side Casey got to work on the vocals. The opening line of the song went 'Mervyn Guy, Mervyn Guy, he's sound of wind and limb, that's Mervyn Guy, he's clear of eye, that's Mervyn Guy'. It was in a marching tempo. I was sitting listening to the song wishing that Casey was singing 'We skipped a light fandango, crossed cartwheels 'cross the floor'. Oh, how different things might have been. We finished the session and began getting everything back into the van as we had a ferry to catch. There was no five-star treatments for us. The producer would mix the tracks later and send the master tapes to Vogue in Germany when they were done. The journey back to Düsseldorf was without incident and I was not optimistic about the record's chances in view of what was charting in Germany at the time. Things had moved on rapidly in Germany from when Casey had had his big hit with 'Don't Ha Ha'. The new record sounded very old fashioned.

And so, it proved to be. It came out a few weeks later and didn't get substantial airplay. Once again recording chart status eluded us and we settled back into our routine in Dusseldorf with a tour to look forward to.

Chapter Seventeen

The next dates in the diary were to be a 10-day tour of Austria. Casey had told us he was still big in Austria, which we all took with a pinch of salt, but it sounded good and we were looking forward to seeing a new country. We had to pack a suitcase each as we were going away for more than a few days and we also decided that if we found somewhere on the way back we would stop and have a few days holiday. We were alarmed that Casey chose to take his high-powered air rifle with him. The holiday looked a good option, as when we got the schedule for the tour they were certainly getting their monies worth out of us. We were scheduled to play 25 towns in 10 days. There were several groups on the tour with us top of the bill. Some shows would be at 2pm in the afternoon, then another town at 4pm and an evening show at 8pm. The first band would go on, play their set, and get their gear off and into the van and on to the next show and so on. It was to be quite a conveyor belt.

We left Dusseldorf on a sunny April day in 1967 and headed for fame and a small fortune in Austria. We were to be met at the border by the promoter, Max Funk, who had a large club in Vienna, called The Chattanooga. When we arrived at the border, there waiting for us was Max with a chauffeur driven Mercedes for our personal use. We left Kurt with the joy of the Transit van and climbed into our luxury limo. Now this was more like it. Max was a nice man and had booked us into some decent hotels and we had twin rooms instead of the large billets we had been used to. The first concert was in Tulln at 6.30 followed by an 8pm show in St. Polten. They were in big Stadthalles which held around 800/1000 people. We were mobbed and treated like stars. The girls screamed and we had police escorts to get us in and out of the theatres. It was scary stuff but we loved every minute of it. The other bands were OK, although we didn't get much chance to see them, as they would always be travelling before or after we had played. They certainly weren't staying in the hotels where we were staying. Travelling around Austria had its moments with Casey, as he would take delight in potting out house windows as we drove along with his rifle. On one occasion we were driving along a mountain pass road which had road works along a stretch of it. When we approached the temporary traffic lights, they were on red. Instead of waiting, Casey jumped out of the car and threw the offending lights into the ravine and told the driver to drive on. We had our knees under our chins until we cleared the stretch of road not knowing whether some lorry was about to meet us head on on the single carriageway which bordered a ravine.

The whole experience was freaky for us, as this had been the first real taste of fame we had had. Each show seemed to get bigger and better and the crowds got wilder and wilder. Halfway through the tour we played a concert in a town called Ternitz at the Stadthalle. It was a big crowd that night and the police were concerned over their safety. I had got hold of a load of damaged drums sticks from a local music store quite cheaply. I used these to throw out into the crowd, as they loved getting something from the band. I threw out a couple of sticks and the kids went wild to get them. The police chief came running up to the side of the stage, puce with rage and told me to stop throwing sticks into the audience. Hey man, I'm a pop star now, you can't tell me what to do at one of our concerts. Wrong. Oh yes, he can. I got carried away and propelled another stick out into the hall as another wave of kids surged to get the memento. As soon as we finished the show the curtains closed and as I walked off, I was grabbed by two burley policemen and bundled into a car and taken to the local station. The Police Chief was shouting at me in clipped English. He was furious that I could have caused a riot and was threatening all sorts. Max arrived and spoke with the Chief for several minutes. Max came to see me and said he had managed to persuade him not to press charges but the Chief wanted me to spend the night in the cells as a punishment. Max said he would come back in the morning early to get me out. I apologised to the Chief for any inconvenience I might have caused him and went off to be locked up. It was not the best night of my life and felt like death. The cell was cold, uncomfortable and smelt of piss with poor toilet and washing facilities. Actually, it reminded me of the hotel in Marburg. I was freed at 7am into the care of Max, who kindly took me to a nice place for a hearty breakfast. The fresh coffee never tasted so good.

One of the final dates of the tour was an open-air concert in a large Sports Stadium in Furstenfeld. There were a lot of people attending this concert and it was packed. The other bands who were supporting us did their respective shows and the crowd had built up nicely. Thankfully the weather was fine and there were around 3,000 fans eagerly awaiting our set. The stage was cleared so we could get all our amps and drums in place and plenty of room to 'mach shau'. We were all ready, in our stage gear and waiting for the compere to announce us. To our disbelief, Casey approached Max and said he wouldn't go on unless he paid him twice as much as he had agreed for this show. He claimed he had only agreed to do clubs and halls and this 'Festival' was a different event involving more people. His argument was that it involved more people and therefore he should get more money. The show had always been in the itinerary, so Casey knew well enough about it. Max was horrified by this blatant blackmail. He was stuffed. If we didn't go on, the crowd would go crazy and there surely would be a riot. There were a few security men around and the odd policeman, but nothing that could contain 3,000 angry fans! He had no choice but to agree. Casey wanted the cash before he played as well. Max went off and soon came back with a wad of money. The look on his face when he handed over the money said a thousand words. We knew Casey would never be booked by Max again. We all felt terrible for Max, as he had been nothing but kind to us all and we really liked him. On we went and went down a storm. Casey was still a 'star' in this part of the world as his records had sold well in Germany & Austria and charted heavily for a few years. They also loved his version of 'Jack the Ripper' which gave them their 'shau' in bucket loads. We ended the concert with this track and the crowd loved it. A few pyrotechnics, bangs and flashes always went down well and we left the stage leaving a happy crowd behind us. We managed to speak to Max later when he was on his own. We apologised to him, but he knew it was not our fault. As we left, he said "At least I can say goodbye to Casey now, you have to stay with him for some time to come". That was a profound statement, as the next few months unfolded, events would take the band in a very different direction.

Chattanooga
ESPRESSO · SNACK · BAR · DANCING · WEINSTUBERL
INHABER MAX FUNK

TOURNEE CASEY JONES & THE GOVERNORS/MIKES & MERLIN/THE CLAN

Freitag, 28.4.:	18.30 Uhr: TULLN, Stadtsaal, Brüderg. 3, Tel.02272/485
	20.00 Uhr: ST.PÖLTEN, Stadtsäle, Völklplatz 1,
	Tel. 02742/2123
Samstag, 29.4.:	14.00 Uhr: HORN, Stadtkino, Thurnhofgasse 14,
	Tel. 310 oder 730
	16.00 Uhr: KREMS, Starclub, Wienerstrasse 24
	Tel. 02732/2480
	22.00 Uhr: FELS/WAGRAM, Gasthof Hegelsberger,
	Tel. 02738/311
Sonntag 30.4.:	14.00 Uhr: AMSTETTEN, Arbeiterkammersaal 1, Wienerstr.55
	Tel. 07427/2626
	17 Uhr: STEYR, Casino, Leopold Werndlstrasse 1c,
	Tel. 07252/2909
	20 Uhr: LINZ, Vereinshaussaal, Landstrasse 40
	Tel. 07222/21662
Montag, 1.5.:	16.00 Uhr: STOCKERAU, Kolpinghaus Tel.02266/2500
	19.00 Uhr: MÖDLING, Brauhauspl., Tel. 02236/2520
	22.00 Uhr: WIEN, Chattanooga, Graben 29 Tel. 52 19 30
Dienstag 2.5.:	18.30 Uhr: EISENSTADT, Hotel Schwechaterhof,
	Tel. 02682/2870 (2101)
	20.00 Uhr: BRUCK/LEITHA, Stadthalle Tel. 257
Mittwoch, 3.5.:	18.30 Uhr: WR.NEUSTADT, Arbeiterheim, Baumkirchnerring
	Tel. 02622/3135
	19.30 Uhr: TERNITZ, Stadthalle, Tel. 02635/8417
Donnerstag, 4.5.:	15.00 Uhr: BRUCK/Mur, Stadtsaal
	17.30 Uhr: KNITTELFELD, Stadtsaal
	19.30 Uhr: FOHNSDORF, Arbeiterheim, Tel. 245
Freitag, 5.5.:	18.30 Uhr: LEIBNITZ, Hugo Wolfsaal
	20.00 Uhr: GRAZ, Arbeiterkammersaal, Hans Reseig. 8-1c
	Tel. 03172/86471
Samstag, 6.5.:	17.00 Uhr: MÜRZZUSCHLAG, Stadtsaal, Tel. 03852/292
	20.00 Uhr: DONAWITZ, Arbeiterkammersaal,
	Tel. 03842/2861
Sonntag, 7.5.:	14.30 Uhr: WEIZ, Volkshaus, Tel. 03172/479
	17.00 Uhr: FÜRSTENFELD, Atus Sportplatz
	20.00 Uhr: SCHACHENDORF, Cafe VANGA, Tel. 03361/20618

Tour intinery for Casey Jones's Austrian tour. I had to keep a copy as no one would believe how many dates we did in such a short space of time!

This incident left a bitter taste in our mouths and none of us were too happy about Casey's attitude. We let the matter drop, as we wanted to enjoy our break after the tour. We were now back in the transit and heading back towards Germany, when we came upon a beautiful hotel overlooking a small lake. After some quick enquiries, they had rooms to spare and we were in the hotel for a couple of days to chill out. The hotel owned a small boat which we were able to borrow to row out into the lake which was great fun. The air was so clean and the weather was mild. For once, we didn't have a care in the world. One afternoon, I had just returned in the boat from a sail around the lake when I noticed Casey along the shore. He stood with his air rifle pointing it towards me. Before I could move I heard the crack as he pulled the trigger and the whizz of the pellet heading in my direction. The pellet hit my forehead. The pain was intense, but luckily it had not penetrated the skin. A lump the size of the pellet immediately sprung up and I realised how different it could have been if it had hit me in the eye. I was furious and went mad with him. We nearly came to blows, as he thought it was funny and he hadn't meant to hit me. I pointed out that he had spent several minutes lining me up in his telescopic sights for it to be an accident.

From that day on my relationship was over with him and I was tired of his stupidity. We all liked a laugh and a joke, but he had to always take it to extremes. The remainder of our stay passed without incident. The rest and good food did us the world of good. We all had time to reflect on our journey so far and how much we had been through. It was sad to leave such a tranquil place, a place that seemed to stand apart from the real world. The drive back to Dusseldorf was a quiet one and no one spoke much, not even Casey.

When we got back to our flat it was apparent that work was not flooding in. It may have been that Max had spread the word around various agents what Casey had done. These guys looked after each other and in terms of the business, what Casey had done was a serious breach of trust between agent and artist. We had money from the tour but by the time we paid Casey the rent it soon started to dwindle. After a couple of weeks and no gigs to do, we realised that things were not good. Every time we asked Casey what was happening he side stepped the issue and said dates would be coming in soon.

His constant arguing with promoters and upsetting them was finally coming home to roost.

As the weeks went buy, the work started to fall away. The three or four gigs a week became one or two and eventually it got down to one gig a month. This had a significant effect on our earnings and suddenly the gold goose was not laying many eggs. Tensions between us were running high as well, as we were hanging around the flat all day living in each others' pockets. We would rehearse in the afternoons, but then we had no money to go out and get a decent meal. The final straw was when we pooled all our money together and we only had enough to buy a big bag of potatoes. This had to last us a whole week. No money, one bowl of potatoes each a day and very few cigarettes. It was about as low as we could get. After the high of supporting The Who and the tour of Austria, this was a bitter come down.

Towards the end of the week, we were all tetchy and one night while we were lying in bed, there was an argument about cigarettes. I had some spare ones, as I had saved my share for such an occasion. Malcolm got the hump and said I should share them around. We were lying in our beds arguing and I wouldn't give in. "We all had the same amount and you smoked yours and I saved mine, so why the fuck should I share them around?" I barked. At that, he lost his temper. He jumped out of his bed, ran across the room and punched me hard in the face. I remember seeing stars. I couldn't believe it. I just lay there and said that as far as I was concerned, when we got back to England, I would not be staying with the band. My nose bled and my head hurt. I was not going to respond, as a fight would have just made matters worse. The boys obviously thought it would blow over, but there was no way I was staying after that. It was a pity his talent for playing the keyboards wasn't up to his talent for pulling girls.

It was all starting to go downhill and we were getting no help from Casey. He was obviously well off and was certainly not struggling for money like we were. While we were surviving on potatoes, he was cooking meals in his side of the flat and the smells that drifted into our room did nothing to allay our hunger or frustrations. On reflection, it was an act of sheer torture to do that to your own band. The man was bereft of morals, compassion and decency. We had made friends with several guys from the main army base and it was now they asked us if we would come and play at their mess one night. We explained we didn't have any transport but they said that was no problem. If we would like to play the following night, they would collect us late afternoon. We couldn't wait, as it meant it was one less night which we would have to spend in our room. It had become our cell and the walls were starting to come in on us. They also promised to feed us.

The following afternoon around 4pm, a 10-ton British Army lorry pulled up outside our flat. It was hilarious. The lorry was massive and out popped two squaddies, who proceeded (at the double) to get our gear in the back of the lorry. The job was done in minutes and we were invited to sit in the back of the lorry as we watched the flat disappear into the distance. After about twenty minutes, we were driving through the main gates of the British Army base at Rheindalen. It was like a large town, hundreds of buildings and lorries, jeeps and every kind of fighting machine moving around like rush hour London. The lorry pulled up outside the mess, which we discovered belonged to the military police. There was a stage in the corner and we got the gear set up as our friends arrived to take us to the NAAFI. This was too good to be true. Proper pork sausages, eggs, chunky chips and lashings of English white bread with butter. All washed down with Typhoo tea; it was like nectar from heaven. We hadn't had a meal so good for ages.

We played several sets during the night and the army guys and their wives loved it. They put a couple of bottles of scotch and a case of coke by the stage and we were set for the night. The lorry duly dropped us off in the early hours of the morning and we slept like babies. They had had a whip round for us and we had at least a few deutschmarks as well for our trouble. We were to repeat these nights over the next few weeks and they were the highlight of our week. On one occasion, after several drinks of scotch and coke, in the last set we were due to play, I counted in the first tune and proceeded to fall backwards off my drum stool crashing to the floor completely pissed. I did somehow manage to finish the set on automatic pilot. After that occurrence, I never had another mouthful of Scotch whiskey again.

Casey had arranged a couple of local gigs in Dusseldorf, which proved how desperate he was. No bookings were coming in from anywhere else and we knew he had gone too far in upsetting promoters. We had had a good chat with our army friends about our predicament. We wanted to get back to the UK, but did not have the transport or the finance to achieve this. The army guys were nothing short of brilliant. A plan was hatched that they would move us out of the flat and two of us would stay with one family on camp and the other two with another. They would then get us some paid gigs around the various army camps, so we could eventually get home. We also approached Kurt, who had been Casey's driver and he was also fed up with not having enough work. He had his own new Ford Transit and was willing to drive us around to the various gigs.

We then had to tell Casey we were leaving him. We knew he was a volatile character and the news did not go down very well. We said we were happy to stay if he could guarantee us work, but he was not willing to do that. We said we were not willing to live on very little money which was making life intolerable. We said we would do the final two gigs he had organised in Dusseldorf and then that was it. On the day of the final gig we were packed and had our cases collected by the army who would take our gear from the gig when we were finished. It would not have been wise to return to the flat after that, as we were not sure what Casey would do. He had been very off with us since we had told him we were leaving.

Performing with Casey Jones in a club in Dusseldorf. (L/R Bob, John, Casey, Arthur)

The final night came and we were in a sombre mood. It was always our desire to play, but this was a time I would have done anything not to do this gig. Our friends from the military police were in abundance and had made it plain to Casey they would not be happy if he started anything with us. At the end of the set we played 'Jack the Ripper' and Casey was lashing into my cymbals with his mike stand, knocking them everywhere. I had a beautiful 22-inch Zildjian cymbal which had the best sound I had ever had and he put a hole right through it. I wanted to kill him. I picked it up and tried to continue, but he just kept smashing it down again. I just threw the sticks down and walked off stage. The army guys who were close to the stage moved forward as the others left the stage as well. Casey was gearing up for a 'My Generation' moment and we were not having any of it.

He came off stage and started having a go at us for not finishing the song. There were lots of pushing and shoving and our army friends made sure none of us got into any trouble. We almost had two minders each. Without them, I believe it would have ended quite badly. We got the gear out as quickly as we could, I almost cried as I put the remains of my cymbal in its case. This was an act of sheer vandalism. We made sure we got our money and we were off without so much as a goodbye. We arrived at our respective army houses and the people made us comfortable. As we settled down in our new homes we reflected on what was in store in the next chapter of our lives.

Chapter Eighteen

Life on the army camp was very different to the flat in Dusseldorf. Here we were being looked after by the wife of the house and it was like being back at home. We would get meals with the family and didn't have to worry about where the money came from. Bob and I were in one house and Malcolm and Arthur were in the other. It was agreed that we would keep a central kitty from the money we earned and the cost of our food would be given to the families. That said, we were being charged no rent, so life was a lot less stressful and we were getting three good meals a day.

We also earned our keep by regularly playing at their mess. The MPs were a hard bunch and one night we got a taste of what they could do. It was local law that German civilians could have access to the messes, which we found very strange strange. However, some local Germans took advantage of this and would go to the mess to drink. There were not many of them and the soldiers hated their presence. I suppose the Second World War was not that old and the older ones on both sides still carried bad memories of the conflict. One of the locals was spotted stealing an ornamental beer stein, putting it in his inside pocket. As they left the building they were stopped and searched. When they found the glass, they grabbed hold of the guy and smashed his head into the edge of a concrete pillar outside the mess. It was horrible. Blood was pouring from the wound and his friends dragged him away and the soldiers just wandered back into the mess for a drink as if nothing had happened. I thought it would be wise to keep on the right side of them!

However, they were doing a great job for us and getting us dates all around the area in various army bases. The money was building up nicely. The jar where it was kept was in our house and it represented our chance to finally get home. We had got some costs of the ferry prices and had also asked Kurt if he would like to take us. He was happy to do the trip, as he wanted to see England and would bring his daughter with him. We never saw Mrs Kurt and never asked if he was still with her. We were always dependent on other people, as none of us could drive.

I had driven the van on a few occasions around Dusseldorf, as I had got a provisional license before leaving the UK the last time we were home. This proved invaluable, as one night, I was driving the van back to the flat after we had had a night out, when we were stopped by the local police. This policeman stepped out onto the road and flashed us down. My heart sank as I eased the van to a standstill by the side of the road. He looked like Rommel. He had a peaked cap, three quarter length dark green leather coat and black boots. I, on the other hand, must have looked like an escaped British evader. I had visions of spending a considerable time in a German cell, as I had in my possession a provisional driving license (not valid for driving abroad) and an out of date insurance cover note (not valid for anything). The policeman asked me for my papers and license. I handed over the offending items and waited for the handcuffs to be applied. His torch shone brightly on the little red booklet that was my license and then the scrap of paper. He looked at me and then the papers, my smile the smile of a dead man walking. 'Alles gut' he said and handed me back the papers. I slid the door shut and drove off as steadily as I could. 'Fuck me boys I need a drink'. Close calls like that were not good for the nerves and we could have been in deep trouble had we been found out.

We were invited to a party on the army camp at someone's house and we got a few cans of lager from the NAAFI and made our way over to the address. There were lots of squaddies there as well as wives, girlfriends and a few local girls for good measure. We were all having a good time when suddenly there was a thudding sound down the stairs, which turned out to be a naked squaddie. He had tried a have sex with one of the girls upstairs and she had turned him down. He had got a bit violent with her and she had not only fought him off but managed to throw him down the stairs as well! Someone called the MPs and we legged it out of the house and ran as fast as we could back to our houses. We had not done anything wrong, but being on the premises after an incident like that, would not have helped our cause to say the least. Thankfully we were out of there before the MPs arrived and were soon home and tucked up in bed.

It was getting to the time when we really did need to get home. Things in the house where Bob and I were getting difficult. The husband had gone away on exercises and it was obvious that the wife was getting frisky, with two young boys in the house. One night I was making myself a late-night coffee in the kitchen when she came in and started to get very friendly. She started to kiss me and things were getting very passionate so I moved quickly into the living room and sat and watched the television with Bob. Suddenly we heard keys being thrust into the front door. It was her husband back from exercises. I was sure I had been here before! Thank goodness, I had taken my leave otherwise I dread to think where that might have left us. Probably bleeding somewhere and nowhere to live. Arrangements and a date were finally made, as it was decided we had enough money for the tickets and the journey. Packing our gear came as a great relief and Kurt came and picked us all up. After what seemed like a lifetime, we were finally off on our way home. It was July 1967.

Kurt had a modern grey Ford Transit van, so we were in much more comfort than the previous journey. The squaddies agreed to get rid of the old Austin J4 van that was on its last legs and we had no way of getting it home. Everything went well on the journey until we got onto British soil. It was obvious Kurt wasn't comfortable driving on the other side of the road. We were cruising up the A1M when he decided to overtake and just ahead of us was a car that had decided to turn right. We were heading straight for the rear end of this car. Everything went in slow motion as we yelled at him about the oncoming hazard. He slammed on the brakes and we came to a halt just as we bumped the car. Unfortunately, our gear had had to be stacked high in the back of the van and a speaker cabinet made its way at speed to those of us sitting behind the driver. It hit our heads with some force and we all shot forward with a bang. Kurt managed to get the van to the side of the road. Those of us in the back were stuck under this great big speaker cabinet. I could feel blood on the back of my neck from the impact but thankfully it wasn't too serious. Finally, with some help from the rest of the group, we got the cabinet from on top of us and back in its rightful place. After a quick check, we were pleased to discover that apart us all having bad headaches, there was no real damage to us, the van or the car in front. It did come as a lesson to Kurt to concentrate a lot more and from there on in, he did get us home safely. The Cock of the North loomed into view as we headed further North; it felt good to be home again. Local agents had already been contacted to inform them of our impending return and we had dates to fulfil. We did not want to return to an empty diary, so it was good to get straight into work mode as soon as we were back.

We also knew that Kurt wanted to see some of the country before returning home, so we couldn't rely on him for transport once we were home. We lined up a driver and a van quite easily from two guys who also had a Transit and were looking for an excuse to get out of the house to go drinking away from their wives!

Deep down, the incident with Malcolm in Dusseldorf was still smouldering away inside me and I was very unhappy. I didn't want to leave, but I couldn't forgive him for attacking me. Had he been a great player I probably would have swallowed my pride, but he wasn't and I thought he had not contributed much to the band. One of our first bookings on our return was at the Seaburn Hall. It was a great venue which held around 1000 people. It was a proper ballroom, right on the sea front which hosted regular dances with two or three bands on the dance night. This evening, we were booked to support a group from Newcastle called 'Toby Twirl'. Originally called The Shades of Blue', they had a good reputation and had just landed a recording deal with Decca Records. The name change came via the recording deal, as Decca had discovered an American band of the same name so they had to change to avoid confusion.

We arrived early evening to set up the gear and each drummer had his own podium either side of the stage. I set up my Ludwig kit and I had to admit it looked wonderful. The stage lights reflected off the grey oyster pearl finish and never have I been so sure I had made the right purchase. When everyone was buying their sparkly Premier kits, I waited and saved that much longer and went for gold. I got up on the podium and let rip; thumping out a beat. I was in top form, having played all the hours in Germany, it was the best possible practice for any musician. The kit seemed to explode with sound and I gave it my all for five minutes and then parked the sticks in the bass drum and went off to the dressing rooms.

I could see some of the members of Toby Twirl having a good look at my playing, but I didn't think anything of it. We played our set and went down well and then came off to watch the top of the bill. I was impressed, as they looked very professional and sounded good with a quality PA. I also noted with interest they had a keyboard player who could play well. After they finished, I was in our dressing room, when I bumped into their bass player, Stuart Somerville. We exchanged pleasantries and completely out of the blue, in a whispered voice, he asked me if I was interested in joining the band. It was almost a repeat of the Beatles story, as their drummer was not rated by their producer, Wayne Bickerton. Their drummer was also getting married and his soon to be bride was not happy about him travelling all over the place, leaving her at home alone. It didn't take long for me to let him know I was more than happy to join the band and gave him my number. The night ended successfully for everyone and we packed up and left for home. I had a good warm feeling that things were about to get better.

A couple of days later I got the call. "Mel Unsworth calling, I manage Toby Twirl. I have arranged a rehearsal tomorrow afternoon at Wetherall's Club in Sunderland to see if you fit in with the boys, is that OK?" "Yes of course" I replied. How do I get there, I haven't any transport?" "Don't worry, I'll pick you up around 1.30 – see you then" Wetherall's Club was a popular night spot in Sunderland owned by the Bailey Organisation, who owned lots of clubs in the North East. Wetherall's had a group night on Mondays and were amenable to let the groups who were playing that night, practise during the day. The following day, I loaded my kit into the boot and back seat of Mel's Jaguar car and arrived at the club with mixed emotions. I was elated at the prospect of playing with a recording group but still sad that I might be leaving Bob, whom I had a lot of respect for and we had been through a lot together.

The boys from Toby Twirl were already there and set up and it didn't take me long to get the kit up with the help of their roadie. The first number they wanted me to try with them was 'Show Me' by Joe Tex. Their old drummer could never master the drum intro and never seemed to get it right as far as they were concerned. This was to be my first test. I knew the number well, as I had performed it many times before. It starts with a one stick roll on the snare into a snappy 4/4 beat and then into the riff. I counted in on the hi-hat and off we went. At the end of the number I knew I was in. I could see the look of satisfaction on their faces. We went through several other tunes and it all fitted in well. I could also do harmonies and had my own mike and boom stand. The best musician in the band was Barrie, the keyboard player, but everyone was more than competent and together they had a very polished sound with good harmony vocals.

Taken during rehearsals at Wetheralls Club, Sunderland just
after joining Toby Twirl

We all sat down and I was told I was in if I wanted the job. I had never done an audition in my life before, so it was a good feeling to 'pass the test'. I was over the moon and they wanted me to start the following week. They wanted to break the news to their old drummer as best they could. It is never an easy job and he was an old friend. I too had to break the news to Bob and although I was delighted to be moving up the ladder, I was sad to be saying goodbye to him. Mel dropped me off at home and I prepared to visit Bob to let him know the news. I walked to his house with a million thoughts going through my head and all those times in Germany and the youth club were flashing like a fast forward replay. I knocked on his door and his Mum answered the knock. Bob's parents had always been great to us and very supportive and seeing her in the doorway with her pinny on, made me feel even worse.

Same rehearsal at Wetherall's Club, Sunderland. Looking happy at being with
my new band – Toby Twirl

As usual, two mugs of piping hot tea and biscuits were produced, as I went into their front room to talk with Bob. His mood was sombre when I told him I was leaving. I explained I could no longer work with Malcolm and this was a chance I couldn't turn down. I said I would see out the gigs that week to give him a chance to find another drummer. Bearing in mind that there were dozens of groups around at the time, it wasn't such a massive task to find someone once the feelers were put out. The remaining gigs were played out low key and no one spoke too much. I certainly didn't speak to Malcolm and he seemed delighted I was leaving.

Chapter Nineteen

So, I was now a drummer in a recording band. We had gigs every single night of the week and it was a roller coaster change. Also, the spread of personnel was immense. Barrie lived in Morpeth; Nick lived in Wideopen, Holly the singer in Blyth, Stuart in Tynemouth and me in Sunderland. It was a 50 mile pick up before we got to a gig! Several of the boys could also drive and had cars, so local for local gigs we tended to go under our own steam. I was now learning to drive as well and expanding on my driving experiences in Dusseldorf. One of the earliest gigs we did was at the Five Bridges Hotel in Gateshead. It was a dinner dance and we were the cabaret. Little did we know that one of the tables was occupied by all the directors of the Bailey Organisation together with their main cabaret booker. We obviously impressed them, as when we had finished, we had a visit to our dressing room. They said they wanted to see us at their main offices in South Shields the following day. Their offices were inside the impressive new night club called La Strada in South Shields situated close to the sea front.

The offices were very posh and we were shown in to John Smith's office. He was one of the main directors together with Stan Henry. His main booker for all the clubs was Myrna Malinsky and they were all there. They came straight out and said they wanted to manage us. We were all flattered and taking into account they owned 26-night clubs, this was quite a negotiating tool when getting us work. There was also the issue of Mel Unsworth, whom we had a management contract with. We were sure Mel would understand and Barrie said he would talk to him after the meeting. Mel did not take the news very well and said he would enforce the contract. He would effectively still collect 15% of all our earnings for the duration of the agreement. We decided that it would have to be, as he was just a local agent and did not have the contacts these guys had. It was Christmas 1967 and we played every night over the holiday period including a lunchtime gig on Christmas day.

Our first single was going to be released on 19th January 1968, so things were moving apace now. The band had recorded three tracks with Decca before I joined the band and the producer had used session musicians. They had just put their vocals on top of the tracks. The three tracks recorded were 'Back In Time' which was written by Wayne our producer and his wife Carole, 'The Fantasy World of Harry Faversham' by some U.S. writers and Utopia Daydream written by Nic, our guitarist. Decca finally decided it would be a 'Double-A' release with 'Back In Time' and 'Harry Faversham'. Our new managers bought us a brand-new Ford Transit Van which was bright red. It was fantastic and unheard of for a group to own a brand-new van. For all our professional lives, we had had to rely on very old unreliable vehicles which, come to think of it, did remarkably well considering all the equipment, people and miles they had to get through. The one thing that filled me with joy was it had a radio and a heater.

Outside the Latino Club in South Shields with our brand
New Ford Transit van – for us it was sheer luxury!
(L/R Stuart, Nick, Barrie, John & Holly)

The next step was to find a permanent road manager to drive it. I knew just the man for the job. Colin Hart had driven the Quandowns; he was working at South Shields town hall and not exactly enjoying life as a civil servant. I contacted Colin and arranged for him to meet the managers. It was very funny, as Myrna auditioned him by getting Colin to drive her around South Shields in the red transit. When he got back to the car park he was offered the job and we were all in place. The next couple of months were to prove decisive for the future of the band. We were all on a wage and the balance was used to pay towards the van and our running expenses. To promote the single, the management decided to send us all over the country into their clubs doing only promotional gigs for the record. So, the wages were going out, but nothing was coming in.

One of the highlights of the single released was being filmed at Bamborough Castle which is on the Northumberland coast. Mike Mansfield, who produced and directed The Tony Blackburn TV Show for Southern television came up with a crew to make the film. The lyrics of 'Harry Faversham' told a story of a damsel in distress being rescued by a knight in shining armour and this made for a perfect promotional film. It was one of the earliest videos of its time. The record did not make the charts, although it got good reviews and by the time we started working again we had incurred 'The Debt' as it became known to us. Thereafter, whenever we tried to get a higher wage or get some money to buy new gear, The Debt was always brought to the table. This had a very detrimental effect on us which ultimately, in my view, led to the eventual break up of the band. We continued to promote and work around the North East throughout the early part of 1968 and working all the time on perfecting our cabaret act, until it was fine tuned into a solid, entertaining and funny show.

For the first single, we also had to drive to London for a photo shoot for Fabulous Magazine. A stylist had gone to King's Road and Carnaby Street and borrowed a selection of clothes for the shoot. We ended up in a photographic studio in the East End of London and felt like proper pop stars. However, the article was published the following week under the banner 'You Don't Have To Be A Pop Star to Wear These Clothes'! So much for instant fame. Nevertheless, it was good for our profile and the radio, television and press we were doing was influencing the live side of our work. The clubs where we were playing were packed full every night. We got a booking at the Top Rank Suite in Sunderland supporting the Small Faces who were right at the height of their career. The hall was packed to the ceiling and the atmosphere was electric. We had great support from the crowd being popular locally and did an hour spot before handing over to the Small Faces. It was interesting to see them arrive in smart mod gear and then appear on stage in T-shirts and jeans.

One of the first 'away' gigs we got to start off our real cabaret career was in Leeds the week commencing 4th August 1968. We were booked to do a double, doing an early show at Kellingley & Knottingley Social club and then a midnight show at The Windmill Club in North Street, Leeds. Part of the booking was that we had to do a lunchtime show at the social club on the Sunday at the start of the week. Being inexperienced, we naively decided to travel after our gig on the Saturday night rather than travel the following morning. To this day, I still cannot understand why we did this. The journey is only 100 miles at most and we pulled up outside the club around 4.30am, beating the milkman by two hours. We all tried to sleep without much success, but at least we were not going to be late. We did the lunchtime and evening show before moving on to the Windmill Club for the midnight spot. On the same bill as us, was a comedian called Tony Dowling who had been doing the club circuit for years. We also had not sorted out where to stay; another strange decision to say the least.

Tony mentioned that he was staying at a place in Roundhay, near Leeds town centre that was not on the 'regular' circuit of show biz digs. He said he would make a phone call and see what he could do. A short while later he came back and said he had persuaded the landlady we were ok and we had accommodation there for the week. What we were to discover was that the rather well-presented house was run by none other than the famous 'Helen Bradley' who had been known to the constabulary of Leeds in her younger days as 'Traffic Light Lill'. Her previous occupation was no mystery and the house was a front for her 'other business'. She ran a show biz digs as a front and you had to be recommended for obvious reasons. We gathered the other business was run somewhere else, but it was a done deal that you didn't answer the phone when it rang. All the rooms were amazing and we were well in. It was not expensive either so a result all round.

Outside the Poco A Poco Club in Stockport where we were top of the bill for the week. (L/R Barrie, Stuart, Nick, Holly & John)

Over the next few years we were to have some great times in this place. We would spend weeks there staying with Freddie Starr and Little and Large who would all try to out do each other. Over cornflakes, you would be entertained to the best cabaret show in the land. At times it was impossible to eat because we were laughing so much. They would constantly try and outdo each other and having breakfast with three Tommy Cooper's was more than enough for anyone. This was our first adventure into the cabaret scene outside of the north-east and it was certainly unusual. However, the rooms were luxurious by comparison and we were happy to take advantage of the situation. I was sharing with Barrie as he didn't smoke and I didn't need that first cigarette in the morning or last one at night. We had the converted garage which was like a Swiss Chalet. Looking back, it was an amazing set up, but I guess the real money was being made elsewhere.

Talking of Tommy Cooper, one of the highlights of this period was playing a week at the Dolce Vita in Birmingham with the great man himself. The Dolce Vita was situated in the Bull Ring, a big shopping complex in the heart of the city and, it was sold out every night. Tommy did not play on the Sunday night, as he would never play on Sundays. Not sure how they managed to get him to do 'Sunday Night at the London Palladium' but that was what we were told. We looked forward to the Monday, and by the time we got to the club, his gear had already arrived. You couldn't move backstage for these huge black cases. Tommy had a stage manager, a very nice middle-aged lady called Kay who looked after his stage clothes and gear. She had some job looking after all his gear. They were all on wheels, so at least they could be moved easily. The cases were rammed with every prop imaginable.

We did our 10 o'clock show and quickly got changed so we could get a prime spot at the back of the club. At midnight, with the club packed to the ceiling, it was time for the great man to entertain. We were not disappointed. After being introduced, the band started its fanfare to welcome Tommy Cooper to the stage – nothing. The band kept playing and the audience were looking puzzled. Suddenly a hand started to push the curtains behind the band, no where near the artist's stage entrance. You could then hear Tommy saying things like 'Where am I?'' and 'Where's the stage?' It is now ten minutes since being introduced and he hasn't even appeared yet. Rumour had it that Tommy suffered very badly from stage fright. He used to use this trick of appearing behind some form of curtains. If he shook the curtains and the audience laughed, he would appear and do his act. If they didn't, he would run back to the dressing room and leave the theatre. He had no problems this week. The audience, not least all of us, were wetting ourselves with laughter. Eventually, his head appeared through the curtains and he clambered over the drum kit and through the band.

The first thing that we noticed was he wasn't wearing his familiar 'Fez' but a bowler hat instead. He apologises for being late and proceeds to do a couple of tricks which fail miserably. The audience are in his hand now. We are holding our sides and we have laughed so much it physically hurts. Several times he complains he has a headache and then nonchalantly takes off the bowler hats and throws it across the stage. The hat lands on the glass floor to the almightiest 'clang'. The hat is made of solid steel. He riffles his hair, says 'That's better' and dons the Fez and proceeds to enthral the audience for an hour and a half. After several encores he is gone. We watch his act for another five nights, and he doesn't do the same thing twice. We can hardly walk by the end of the week with laughing so much, but it was an experience we will never forget. One of the true comic greats and it was a privilege to have played along side him.

We travelled next to Southport in Lancashire for the next week's work. Southport was a typical English seaside resort, I am sure in summer it is a lovely place. However, we always seemed to end up there in the middle of winter. It was grim. Most places were boarded up for the winter and nothing seemed to be open apart from the Kingsway Casino, our home for the next seven days. The club owner owned a Bingo Hall elsewhere in the town and as the Casino was closed on Sundays, the club owner had the acts perform at the

Bingo Hall instead. It was a converted theatre so it had a nice big stage and good lighting.

The punters sat and played a few games of bingo and then the comedian would go on and do half an hour. Then a few more games and it was our turn to entertain. Being the drummer, I was set up at the back of the stage with the old Marshall stacks either side. About half way through our act, the audience all started to get to their feet and rush towards the front of the stage. I thought all these old age pensioners were going to attack us. I was scared witless. However, the boys at the front of the stage didn't seem to be worried, so I kept on playing. What I hadn't seen was the theatre staff that had appeared into the orchestra pit in front of the stage and started to serve steak pies, mushy peas and mash. Part of the entrance fee for the punters was a free pie and pea supper and this lot were not going to wait for us to finish our act before tucking in to their grub. Talk about the expression 'Pies have come', on that occasion they truly had.

We slowly established ourselves onto the cabaret circuit and before long we were working the clubs around Manchester and Leeds on a regular basis. Two of the most popular clubs at the time were the Princess and Domino clubs in Manchester and we would do a 10pm spot at the Domino and then move on to do the midnight cabaret at the Princess. The club scene in those days was fantastic and every night there would be a good crowd in to entertain. The days of discos had not yet appeared and many clubs subsidised their cabaret club by their casinos. During a week we were playing in Manchester at the Domino, we had just started out show when we spotted what was obviously a group make their way to a table half between the bar and the stage. You could just tell they were musicians and not ordinary punters out for night on the town.

Shortly after we finished, there was a knock on the dressing room door. There they were, asking if they could come in for a chat. They were from London and were starting out in the cabaret scene and had come to see us to get an idea of what was expected. They were a good bunch of lads and we got on well with them straight away. Their name was 'Mud'.

They were also looking for accommodation and we were staying at Stevenson's Hotel in Whalley Range. In those days it was a legendary place and all the groups playing in the Manchester area would stay there. The bedrooms were very much the 'family' room I had been used to in Germany with four beds in each. From then on, we would see Mud on a regular basis and we ended up playing five a side football in the local park in the afternoons to keep fit. The heating in the rooms was usually an electric fire which had a meter attached to it. I am sure Mr. Stevenson had doctored the meter because as soon as you put a coin in, the dial would revolve round like a 78rpm record and the fire would go out five minutes later.

One night, for some reason, we did not have a late show to do and we knew Mud were playing at the Princess Club at midnight. After playing our early show, we headed over to the Chorlton club in Barley Moor Road. I noticed it was just down the road from a huge cemetery so no problem if you died on stage! We had already phoned the club and arranged for us to get in OK as we were regulars. We were shown to our table and ordered a round of drinks and some chicken in the basket. We were well set. Just after midnight the lights dimmed and on stage came the compere, illuminated by a follow spot. After a few quick jokes he introduced the top of the bill – 'Ladies and Gentleman, please give a big hand for tonight's star turn – Mud'.

On stage came our mates and they went straight into their first song. One song followed another, all sounding strangely familiar, not least some of the patter in between. We all looked at each other with some amazement and Stu, in a stage whisper said, 'Fuck me boys, they've nicked our act'. Les Gray obviously heard what Stu had said and looked sheepishly through the lights and spotted us. After they had finished their act, a rock n' roll medley and a parody of Elvis a la Toby Twirl, they left the stage to good applause. After a short while we went backstage and pretended to be real mad at them. They hadn't just taken a couple of numbers but used our whole act! They were very apologetic and looking highly embarrassed. Suddenly, we couldn't keep our laughter in any longer and we all had a good chuckle about it. They did promise to change it, which they did after a few weeks and firmly established themselves on the circuit.

They mentioned they were going back to London at the end of the week to meet two songwriters who wanted them to record a couple of tracks they had just written. The writers were Mike Chapman and Nicky Chinn and the one of the tracks was song called 'Crazy'. The record was released on Mickie Most's RAK label and they had great chart success for several years. From then on they left the cabaret scene to tour extensively at major concerts. We were delighted that they had got success, but it felt like another chance had slipped us by.

One week, we did the legendary Embassy Club in Manchester, the club owned by the comedian - Bernard Manning. His mother worked behind the bar and the banter between Bernard and his mother was hilarious. It was certainly an experience and a hard school to learn your craft. People accuse him of being racist and politically incorrect but the one thing about Bernard was no one escaped his humour whatever you were. I turned up one day in striped blazer type jacket (see photo of us entering the Playboy Club) as we strolled towards the artist's dressing rooms. Bernard spotted me as he was on stage at the time and said, 'Look out lads, there's a fucking anaconda just entered the building.'

We were now established on the Northern cabaret scene and working 52 weeks a year in and around the country. During a week working at the Poco a Poco in Stockport, our A&R manager from Decca, Wayne Bickerton, came up to see us in our hotel to play us potential follow up tracks. Wayne had been writing with his long-time partner Tony Waddington and they had written a track called 'Romeo & Juliet 68' with the lyric based on Shakespeare's play. Nicky and I had also written a track called 'Toffee Apple Sunday' which was inspired by the fun fair at Whitley Bay called Spanish City where we had spent many afternoons. It was decided that we would record both these tracks at our next recording session.

After Wayne returned to London, he spoke to our management and a date was set for us to travel to London to record the two songs. This time it was decided that we would do all the recording and only session musicians would be used for brass and strings if required. This was a great confidence boost from Decca as to our musicianship but filled us with complete terror. The recording studio to us at the time was a totally alien environment and one that we had rarely set foot in.

We set out from the North East to Decca's West Hampstead studios, again leaving at some ungodly hour to travel the 300 hundred miles so we would arrive at lunchtime. We piled into a Chinese restaurant opposite the studios to have lunch, as we were all starving having almost travelled through the night to get there on time. The session was due to start at 2pm and end at 5pm. In those three precious hours we would have to record the backing tracks and vocals for the two songs. Our gear was loaded into studio 3, the smallest studio at the complex and we set up for recording. It did not pass our attention that the Moody Blues were recording in Studio 1, the studio usually used for symphony orchestras, as they were doing an oboe overdub. It was clear then where we stood in the pecking order!

For me it was a nightmare. My drums were totally geared for live work and it was obvious the engineers were used to session drummers turning up with drum kits ready to be recorded. With so little time to do everything I had to do a quick learning curve on how to doctor the kit so it would be ready for recording. With Wayne and Tony in the control room, assisted by Adrian Varnells as engineer, and a certain Gus Dudgeon (later to become Elton John's producer) as tape operator, we played out the first take. Wayne asked if I could do a drum intro which no one had asked me for before. Sitting behind the kit looking up at the faces behind the control room window, I felt like being a defendant in the dock at the Old Bailey. I was terrified that if I screwed up, it could be the end of our recording deal. So much for a laid back creative environment! The session thankfully went well and we did both tracks in the three hours. The drum intro was recorded for posterity on 'Romeo & Juliet 68'. Of course, recording could not come in the way of live work and after the session we drove from London to Birmingham to do a gig at the Dolce Vita at midnight. Hard to think these were the days when bands were going off to retreats to get inspiration for their forthcoming recordings.

Our second single was released and Decca decided to make 'Toffee Apple Sunday' the A-side. This came as a big surprise and there was a certain jealousy in the band as other members thought Nicky and I were about to make millions. Once again, we were denied decent air play by Radio 1, even though we were regularly recording sessions for them. Several times a year, we would go to the BBC's Manchester studios where John Wilcox would produce five tracks with us and these would be played one a day on Radio 1 and repeated a few weeks later. Occasionally we would do a Radio 1 Road Show, which entailed playing live on air which, of course, had its own share of nightmares. We played one of these shows at the Top Rank Suite in Preston where Stuart Henry was the DJ. We set up all our gear and the engineers wanted all our speakers at the front of the stage so they could mike them up easier. That was all well and good until the crowd flooded in and made their way to the front of the stage knocking over the microphones in the process. It was hell for me as the speaker cabinets all had sealed backs, so I couldn't hear anything other than the sound bouncing off the back of the hall. All this of course was going out live on Radio 1.

During a week's cabaret at The Bailey Club in Sheffield, we took to the stage as usual. We were very professional and had devised a way of starting our act without us all walking on to the stage at the same time, plugging guitars in and the usual racket that ensues. Most cabaret stages were surrounded by tables where the audience would sit and drink and dine during the evening. When the stage lights went out, I would slip on to the drums at the back of the stage. When I was in position, the compere would announce us and a spot would hit me on the drums. I would start laying a beat quickly followed by Stu on bass, Nick on guitar, Barrie to his keyboards and the finally Holly in front of the lead mike. As each of us came on stage, the lighting would slowly get brighter until we had full lights and then once Holly was in place we would go straight into 'Fools Rush In' segued by 'Up Up and Away'. This night, as Nick walked on the stage, he plugged in his guitar, turned to the front of the stage and with one hand on the fret board holding the chord of G; he straightened his microphone with the other. Suddenly all hell broke loose. There was an electrical fault somewhere in the system and by touching the mike, he had formed a circuit. The subdued lighting only made it look more dramatic and Nick was paralysed, unable to let go of the mike. I could clearly see a bright blue arc around his body which was totally shocking. People in the crowd were screaming and Holly, with great reactions, booted the microphone stand away from Nick. Nick crashed to the floor of the glass stage motionless.

We were terrified he was dead. Colin was now on stage and we were trying to get Nick conscious. Thankfully he started breathing and the manager of the club had already called the ambulance service. They were on sight in good time and took Nick away to be treated. By the time they took him away, we knew he was going to be OK, as he made some sort of joke as they loaded him into the ambulance. His hand had burns where he had been holding the guitar and the strings were welded on to the fret board for the chord of G! Of course, we had to take the piss and tell him later it would not be a problem as it was the only chord he really knew. What was awkward for us was that the club was owned by our managers. They brought in inspectors to test the gear and their circuitry and of course, nothing was proven to be faulty. Ultimately, we were just thankful Nick was OK and he was back on stage two days later. We did notice he did not touch his mike for weeks.

After months of travelling the country doing weeks of cabaret, our managers told us that we had been booked to do a tour of Germany doing U.S. Air force bases near Frankfurt. None of the boys had been to Germany before, so I was the senior pro here! It would be very different this time in as much as we were not working civilian clubs, so the hours would be a lot more normal than when I had been there previously. It would be a lot more comfortable going there this time too. A new Ford Transit van with airline seats was a good start. We would also drive to Hull and then ferry to Rotterdam which was much easier than all the way to Dover.

In a strange way, I was looking forward to going back to Germany. Especially given the more comfortable form of transport we had. The ferry port at Hull seemed to be much bigger than Dover. It was certainly a lot less gruelling than driving so far south; to then have to drive so far North on the other side of the Channel. At first, we got lost trying to get out of Rotterdam, but eventually we found the right road and we were soon on the motorway. We ended up on the E41 autobahn which seemed to be strangely familiar. I remember, as we drove down this autobahn towards Frankfurt, I suddenly felt an uneasy feeling and began to turn cold. I thought I was going to feint. I looked out of the window of the van and immediately saw the motorway sign which said 'Marburg'. My blood ran cold as I saw the spire of the Cathedral standing on the hill and I could feel the cold stone floor Bob and I had kneeled on to pray that we would be saved that dark day in 1966.

With some relief we drove further south towards Frankfurt where we were to play at the most enormous air force base. Accommodation was a small hotel nearby which was basic but clean. We were also told that we could have access to their mess which meant lots of good food at very cheap prices. The first gig was to be in an enlisted men's mess. The hall was massive and must have held over 1000 GI's. The first problem was that these guys wanted to see a girl singer with big tits, not five blokes from the North East of England.

The other issue was more complex. Standing on the stage you could draw a line down the middle of the hall. On the left-hand side were all the white guys who wanted country music and on the right were all the black guys who wanted soul. There we were stuck in the middle trying to please them all. To say it was hard work as an understatement. We persevered on and managed to finish the night without being lynched. The following days were much better as we played mostly officers clubs. The officers could have their wives in attendance, so the atmosphere was much more convivial to our style. It was a good trip though which ended well with a drunken night at the base before heading back to the UK and more cabaret dates.

One highlight was to do a week at the famous Batley Variety Club. In a small mining village just outside of Leeds was this cabaret club. It was the size of an airplane hangar. We were booked on the same bill as Ray Martine and Anne Shelton who had made their name on the popular programme 'Stars & Garter'. A variety show based on in East End Pub. Apparently legend has it that the first programmes were recorded in the real Stars & Garter, but there was so much trouble in the pub, they had to make a set in the television studio for future episodes. It was strange to arrive in a small place and discover this huge building that was bigger than the town! As usual, the week started on the Sunday and after load in and sound check, we settled in our dressing room. At around 7pm I wandered out to the side of the stage and peered through the curtains. The hall was soft lit and each table had a table lamp. There were hundreds of tables leading to the back of the hall where there was a large bar area. Unfortunately, all the tables were empty.

However, the bar staff were pulling endless pints and stacking them in long lines. I made my way back to the dressing room and told the boys about the empty room. There is nothing worse than playing to an empty room, especially one that is so big. At 7.30pm I wandered back to see if there was any improvement. I was shocked to see a complete full house! What we had not realised of course, was that most of the people coming to Batley travelled by coach and they all turned up the same time. Hence the mass pint pulling before they arrived. Chicken or Scampi in the basket was a big favourite too.

It was great to play at Batley as it was run like a proper theatre. The stage lighting was very good and they had two spot lights operated from the back of the room. The house band was big and had around 16 musicians. They had a big brass section which was led by Red Price, the legendary sax player with Lord Rockingham's Eleven. We had a great week with Anne Shelton getting everyone going with her popular songs and ending off with a rousing version of her hit 'Lay Down Your Arms & Surrender To Me' whilst waving a huge Union Jack flag. We would do our show in between before Ray Martine closed the show with his unique comedy act.

Ray's humour was a blend of Jewish and East End comedy. His famous gag which he ended on most nights was the story of the world-famous gourmet who visited this famous restaurant in the West End of London. He selected his main course which was listed as Aylesbury Duck. Eventually the maitre d' brought this large silver platter. Presenting it at the table, he removed the lid and with some flourish announced 'Monsieur, your Aylesbury Duck'. The gourmet pulled up his sleeve, stuck his finger up the parson's nose and informed the maitre d' that this was in fact Wiltshire Duck. Would he be so kind as to bring him an Aylesbury Duck immediately? Ten minutes later another silver platter arrived and the same routine ensued. After plunging his finger up the parson's nose, the gourmet announced that the duck this time was Staffordshire Duck, please bring me an Aylesbury Duck. By this time the maitre d' was red with rage and faces began appearing through the kitchen door. After a short while, the head chef appeared with another silver platter. 'Monsieur, finally your Aylesbury Duck'. After sticking his finger up the parson's nose, the gourmet announces with some delight that it is indeed an Aylesbury Duck. He then enquires what part of France the Chef came from. The Chef drops his trousers, bends over, and says 'You tell me Monsieur, you're the bloody expert'.

We would end our act with a rock n' roll medley and after a couple of nights, we were just into the start of the medley and I noticed Red Price and his brass section had wandered on stage and were blowing a storm with us. It was fantastic to have their brass sound and they joined us on stage for the rest of the week.

On our return to the North-East, our management called us to their offices for a meeting. We were slightly reticent and thought we had done something wrong. It was not the first time we had been on the end of a ticking off! Recently we had performed at a working men's club in Wallsend and had gone down a storm. By the time we came off stage it was 10.50pm having played several encores. The concert secretary, well happy, had left the building. We were towelling off in our dressing room and Colin was packing up the gear. In comes the Chairman of the club and tells us we must be out of the club by 11.00pm. Well, that was the thanks we got for going down well. He kept going on and on at us, so we all quickly changed and helped Colin load the van. Something we did not normally do (apart from the Hammond organ). He stood by the emergency doors still moaning at us for taking so long so I told him to 'Fuck off and stop being such a prick'. Always the diplomat! The next day he called our managers and we were summoned and duly told we were expected to behave. So, we all arrived for the meeting and piled into Myrna Malinsky's office and held our breath.

We were instantly calmed when she obviously saw we were bemused by what we had done. She explained that she had had a call from Marcel Stellman, a top executive at Decca, who wanted us to sing the theme song to a new major movie which would star David Niven and Eli Wallach. They had arranged a date for the session at Decca's London studios. The film was called 'The Brain' and the main song as also of the same name. Myrna played the demo and it certainly wasn't 'You Only Live Twice' but it might just lead to greater things. After the meeting we all met up in the Latino car park and unanimously agreed the song was crap but we couldn't turn down the opportunity.

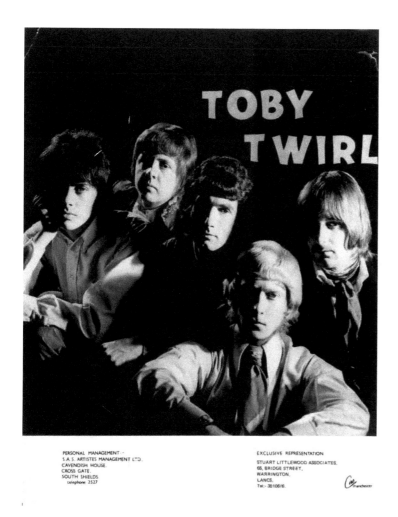

Early publicity shot for Toby Twirl with original line up
(L/R Holly, Barrie, Nick, John & Stuart)

We duly arrived at Decca's offices on the Thames and were met by Marcel Stellman. He was a lovely guy and obviously had a lot of experience in the film and recording industry. He took us into a rehearsal room on the ground floor where he had booked a piano player, so we could routine and work out harmonies. The keyboard player was Nicky Hopkins, a top session player who had played with The Stones, The Who, David Bowie and just about everybody else at the time. We managed to crack the arrangement and Marcel was finally happy with our harmonies. After a quick spot of lunch, we drove over to West Hampstead for the vocal session. To our surprise, we were in Studio 1, the Moody Blues must have been on holiday! We had the vocals down without much problem in about an hour and everyone seemed pleased with the result (if not the song). We were soon on the road back to Newcastle as worked beckoned the following day.

Some months later, we noticed 'The Brain' playing at a local cinema in Leigh, near Warrington where we were in cabaret with Kiki Dee. The ultimate ego trip going to the cinema and hearing your own voices coming through the sound system as the film got going. There only seemed to be us in the cinema as the curtains parted and the film rolled. On came the opening tune 'The Brain' and we all looked at each other in shock. It wasn't us! Somewhere along the line our version must have been ditched and they got someone else to do it and no one had bothered to tell us. We were totally shocked and left the cinema in disgust. So much for our international movie career – more Brooke Bond than James Bond. Later that night we all had a good laugh about it over a pint and given how rubbish the song was, decided it was better our name wasn't associated with such a turkey after all.

Later that year we got booked to do a week at the Pavilion Theatre, Bournemouth. Topping the bill was Kathy Kirby, whose big hit was 'Secret Love' and guest star was Solomon King, who was in the charts with a song called 'She Wears My Ring'. It was a real seaside show with all sorts of speciality acts. We did two shows a night, one at 6pm and another at 8.30pm. We opened the show with three numbers and that was our lot! It was an easy week, but good experience working in a theatre rather than the cabaret clubs. Solomon King used to invite us into his dressing room for a game of Scrabble which he loved to play. He was a very big man and was 6' 8" tall. Unfortunately, he would insist on sitting in just his large underpants to play Scrabble which was a bit unnerving. He would really wind us up by insisting on putting down words that were clearly American slang like 'Whup'. Our love of board games diminished somewhat as the week progressed. As we finished early, we were able to slip around the corner to the beat club which was part of the theatre complex on the Friday night to watch Chicken Shack. Their lead guitarist was the legendary Stan Webb and on keyboards was Christine Perfect who would later join Fleetwood Mac and become Christine McVie. Listening to her version of 'I'd Rather Go Blind' in such a small intimate club was inspiring. I think she was a much-underrated vocalist at the time.

Shortly after that, we found ourselves in Sheffield doing various clubs around the area for a week. We had to cancel the Friday night show because we all had cold and lost our voices. We were hopeful that medication we had got from a local doctor would sort us for the Saturday night show. We couldn't afford not to work as no work, no money! As it was Friday, it seemed a shame to stay in our digs, so after our evening meal, we took ourselves into Sheffield town centre to the Cavendish Club, another Bailey owned club. Of course, everyone on the Bailey Club circuit knew us, so getting a table was no problem.

We were delighted that topping the bill was a jazz funk trio called The Peddlers. Roy Phillips on organ, Trevor Morais on drums and Tab Martin on bass. They were very popular in clubs and their musicianship was top notch. Roy did the vocals and had a Ray Charles quality in his voice. Their show was also very entertaining and we were looking forward to their midnight performance. We had made friends with them, as we had played together on shows a few times, especially Trevor, who had a wicked sense of humour. The club by now was heaving, absolutely packed to the rafters. It was Friday night in Sheffield and all the steel workers were downing pints of lager, as if it was an Olympic sport. By the time 10pm arrived, it was rowdy to say the least. On the table it had printed on the menus, which acts were appearing at the club over the coming weeks. We noticed for this particular week, the act supporting The Peddlers, was a Scottish comedy duo called 'McNeil & Trotter. This was going to be interesting. As it turned out, we were about to witness one of the funniest things you are likely to see in any club or theatre.

As usual, the resident band's drummer did a drum roll and cymbal crash and on came the compere to introduce the 10 o'clock show. He was struggling to get the audience's attention, but like a trooper, battled and finally almost shouting, announced 'Ladies & Gentlemen, please give a warm Sheffield welcome to McNeil & Trotter. The band struck a lively tune and arms linked, on to the stage came the mighty Scottish duo. They had the full gear on, kilts, long socks (with requisite dagger), and sporrans and of course tamashanter hats. Just as they got to the centre of the stage a huge bloke with a massive beer belly stood up near the front of the stage, cupped his hands round his mouth and shouted, 'Fuck off'. It this point, McNeil & Trotter immediately switched arms and danced off the stage, never to be seen again. I don't think many of the crowd really noticed what had happened. We were under the table in tears of laughter; the muscles in my stomach were aching. They had obviously decided to cut their losses and quit whilst they were ahead. Probably a very good decision under the circumstances.

One of our favourite clubs was the Cavendish Club in Blackburn. It was one of the new Bailey Clubs to be built. It was very large and had two cabaret rooms in the same building as well as a casino. Each act performing there would do a 10 o'clock show in one lounge and then swap for the midnight show. We also loved Blackburn because we had found a good place to say. The landlady's name was Anne, and she was obviously on her own. It turned out her husband had died, so she had turned her house into a guest house to make ends meet. She was a lovely lady and made us very welcome. We were always well behaved, as at first, she was worried having a 'group' stay with her. We were not going lose a good place through bad behaviour, as these places were like gold dust. The first time we stayed there, we sat down for dinner with great anticipation, as she had told us we were having home made steak and kidney pie. After having soup, she came through with the pie and put it in the middle of the table. It wasn't very big and I could see everyone cutting it into six with their eyes and realising that what was left was not a very big portion. She was to have the last laugh, as she proceeded to bring in another five pies the same size. We were stuffed, but the food she made was outstanding every time we stayed there.

We did a week in Blackburn with Lonnie Donegan and his band. We did not know what to expect his act to be like as we just knew him as a skiffle player. He was a brilliant entertainer and exceptional banjo player and used to do an amazing duet with his guitarist at the time, Les Bennett. Les was a real character and had a very dry sense of humour. One evening we were sitting having a quiet drink in the small cabaret lounge before many punters had arrived at the club. He came over and sat with us a while and as our glasses were getting empty, he said 'Come on lads, I'll buy you all a drink'. Well, we were up like a shot and at the bar in record time. Six lagers ordered and we looked round – Les had vanished!

On our way into the Playboy Club in Park Lane to play a set to promote 'Movin' In'. (L/R Holly, John, Nick, Barrie & Stuart)

Our third Decca single 'Movin' In' was scheduled for release in January 1969. To promote the single, it was arranged that we would do our act at the Playboy Club in Park Lane and Decca and our PR would invite radio, press and television producers to let them see us and show what we could do. On the 7th January we took the long drive down to London again, leaving in the early hours. It was important to get there mid afternoon so we could set up for the early evening performance. The set went well and the radio producers and journalists liked the fact that we could entertain as well as just play. Of course, being what we were, after taking plaudits for our performance, we loaded up the gear and headed off for a midnight cabaret in the Midlands. Sadly, the ever-elusive Radio 1 playlist turned its back on us again and the record failed to make the charts. Our recording career was now doomed and Decca did not renew our recording contract. We would never make another record.

Frustrations were also setting in as we were working 52 weeks a year, topping the bill everywhere we went, but because of the 'debt' our wages were not great and singers supporting us on the bill were getting three times as much as we were. Holly was also smoking and drinking a lot, which was fine, except it was affecting his voice. Holly had a good voice and it recorded very well as our early recordings show. It all came to a head one night when he couldn't hit certain notes and then after the show went off to smoke loads of cigarettes and down a few pints.

TOBY TWIRL

PERSONAL MANAGEMENT
S.A.S. ARTISTES MANAGEMENT LTD.
CAVENDISH HOUSE
CROSS GATE
SOUTH SHIELDS
telephone 2527

Last publicity shot of Toby Twirl before Stuart was drowned in a canoe accident off Tynemouth
(L/R Nick, Barrie, Stuart, John & Steve P

It was decided he would have to be replaced, which was a major move for the band. Our agent at the time was Stuart Littlewood and he recommended a guy from Rochdale called Steve Pickering. Steve had been playing in a band under the name Reg James and had a good following in the North West. We arranged to meet up with him and try a few tracks and it seemed to work well. Finally, Holly had to be told it was over for him. It is such a horrible thing to do as groups are very tight knit units. The move was made and we rehearsed our cabaret act together with some new numbers that Steve had made his own with his other band. Cabaret dates went well and Stuart managed to get us a 10-day tour of Denmark. Steve had previously been over there with his own band and had established a good reputation. It was September 1969.

We left on a ferry from Newcastle, which was very handy although when we arrived on the quayside, there was no sign of a way to drive the van with all our equipment on board the ship. It was only then we realised that it would have to be lifted on by a crane! We all stood there and watched as our beloved new red transit van ascended into the sky, swinging around in the wind towards the hold of the ship. One of the straps slipped from the front wheel and it lurched precariously, our hearts in our mouths as it slowly descended to safety into the hold. That was a moment we would not forget in a hurry. Sailing down the Tyne was quite an experience and watching the pier at Tynemouth disappear as we headed for Esbjerg. The journey was spent having several beers before disappearing for a restless night in our cabins. It was an early rise as we docked in the morning and thankfully the van was exhumed by the Danes from the hold without any problems. We were all excited about this trip as we all knew how nice Danish girls were. When I say we were 'all' excited about Danish girls, this sadly didn't include Barrie. Poor old Barrie had caught a dose of the clap a couple of weeks before we were due to go to Denmark. So, while we were looking forward to sampling some good home brewed Carlsberg and lovely blonde Danish girls, Barrie was in for ten days of penicillin and orange juice.

We had to drive to Copenhagen for our first gig, which was to be at the famous Revolution Club. Denmark is made up of three islands and each island is connected by ferry. A minor detail our management had not considered as the ferry costs were quite high. By the time we had finished our tour, ferry costs had almost swallowed most of our profit. We also discovered that Steve had a girl friend in Copenhagen and he would be staying with her. That would save him some hotel costs. The first night we met Hannah and she brought a friend with her who was nice. We got on very well and I was invited to stay at Hannah's flat, so we could enjoy a night together. I ended up staying there for the week we were in Copenhagen which saved me some hotel costs as well.

The Revolution Club was good and the audience were OK although we found them very hard to please. The one thing that impressed us was the huge in-house speakers that blasted out records in stereo. Clubs in England did not have sophisticated sound systems, as their main source of entertainment was groups. It struck me at the time that this would have a significant effect on live music in the future. After four nights at the Revolution we had to drive to Aarhus for our next gig, which was on the first island. The countryside was good and the ferries comfortable so there was no hassle with the travelling. We stopped at a farm to buy some milk which was ice cold and seemed to taste like nectar out of bottles that were dark brown. I think Danish dairy products had had good publicity prior to our trip and we were already in a zone with its quality.

Aarhus is Denmark's second largest city and we were due to play at a large sports hall on the outskirts of the city. The hall was medium sized and again the audience were good but still hard to please. We went down well in the end and had a good night at our hotel and partied into the early hours with Hannah, Karyn and some other girls whom the boys had managed to invite back to the hotel. It was back to Copenhagen again for a few nights before the long journey back to Esbjerg and then the sea trip to Newcastle. It was at this point that Steve asked if we could bring Hannah back to the UK with us. It was a hard call, as the van comfortably seated 6 but not 7. We eventually agreed and Steve had Hannah sit on his lap for most of the way. Some of us felt it was the first time he'd put himself out for anything.

The arrival back at Newcastle was without drama and poor Colin had the joy of dropping us all off at our respective homes before he could settle down to a welcome cup of English tea. We had a full diary of cabaret bookings to take us into Christmas and we were pleased to see that over Christmas, we were working locally which was good news indeed. At Christmas we would be doing a double with working men's clubs first and then a midnight cabaret at The Sand's Club in Whitley Bay. It was here that we would renew our acquaintance with Freddie Starr. After the first working men's club we arrived at Sand's Club around 11.30pm and it was all hands to the pump as we had to get all the gear into the club and ready to play at midnight. I grabbed all the stage suits and took them up the stairs to the dressing rooms. I was aware there was someone in the room as I started to hang up the suits. A voice behind me enquired 'What do you think of this?' I turned to see Freddie Starr standing at the back of the room with his penis in his hand. Trying to act cool I replied, 'Very nice' and legged it back to the van. For once, carrying the gear into the club didn't seem such a chore. When we eventually made it back to the dressing room, Freddie and his one-eyed friend had gone.

We eventually bade farewell to the sixties as the decade ended and we moved into 1970. The frustration with the 'debt' continued to fester and the more we saw solo artists supporting us but making twice as much as us, took the edge off our popularity.

We were booked to play at a working men's club in Middlesbrough one Sunday evening and as usual the van arrived outside my house in Sunderland around 5.30pm. As I was the last to be picked up going south, I always got the dodgy seat in the back. I noticed Stu wasn't in the van but his brother was. His brother often came along to gigs to help Colin with the gear. I was told Stu had gone to a party after the gig the previous night and hadn't got back until early morning. Apparently, as it had been a lovely summer's morning with the sun up early, he had taken his canoe out for a ride. We were told he would be following on later.

We arrived at the club and the boys began setting up the gear. Colin went to find a phone to call Stu's parents. When he came back he had the look of a ghost. They had found Stu's canoe and life jacket (which he'd used as a seat) but no sign of Stu. This did not look good. We discussed our options in the dressing room and decided there was no way we could perform that night under the circumstances. We all put on a brave face, not least for his brother, and explained to the club our problem. They understood our predicament and the journey back was made in silence with the odd 'Don't worry, you know Stu, he'll show up looking like a sack of shit!' I was first to be dropped off and the van sped off down the road. I had a bad feeling that the outcome of this was not going to be good and would have long term implications for the group.

The following morning, I rang Stu's house and was told there was still no sign of him. The coastguard and police had been alerted and they had had the North Sea Rescue service searching the coast without any success. Later that day, we all went to Stu's house to offer our support. Stu's parents were great people and they had been a big part of the group, always supportive and friendly. They never found his body. This must have been very upsetting for his family, as there was no real closure. Stu was a real character and being a founder member of the group, it left a big hole. The group was very much like a family, living in each others' pockets, seven days a week, so the loss was great. The first few gigs we did without a bass player to fulfil commitments, and when we did 'Girls' which he would normally sing, we all choked with tears running down our faces.

We auditioned for a bass player the following week and eventually offered the job to Dave Robson. Dave lived in Gosforth and had a similar sense of humour to us so he fitted in well. We all did not realise just how much a part of the group Stu had been. It felt like the stuffing had been totally knocked out of us. We were still as popular in the clubs and the bookings were still there with a full diary. We also had a feeling that Steve was making plans to leave us. Our agent, Stuart Littlewood, seemed to be working behind the scenes for him. This was something we had picked up on the cabaret grapevine.

After another six months of endless cabaret, we decided to call it a day. Without a hit record we were never going to elevate the band to a certain level where we could have earned really good money, so it was probably the best time to go. Our last night was at a club in Hartlepool, hardly the Vegas of the North! We all went through the motions and it was a sad journey back down the A19 to home. Taking the drums out of the back of our lovely red transit for the last time was a sad experience. It could all have been so different. It was a hell of a journey I had made so far and I was only 22.

Barrie and Nick formed a duo and continued to work the clubs until Nick decided to become a social worker. Barrie continues to this day to work the clubs and cabaret circuit. Dave went on to form another group called Fogg whom I helped to manage and we got them a deal with EMI and Warner Brothers Records. Dave now manages the Big Market in Newcastle upon Tyne. Steve, who thought we weren't trendy enough, changed his name to Dudley Doolittle and became a comedian. Something we still find hard to believe to this day. How untrendy is that? Holly found his Nirvana by managing a pub called the Blyth Arms. Colin went on to roadie for Deep Purple all over the world and now lives in Florida.

As for me, I did a residency in a local working man's club and got a job with Granada Television Rental, finally managing their shop in Durham City. Then one day I got a call from a music publisher in London, who wanted to see me about a job.

That, of course is another story!